GATHERED IN TIME

GATHERED IN TIME

Utah Quilts and Their Makers,

Settlement to 1950

A UTAH QUILT HERITAGE BOOK

Kae Covington

WITH A HISTORICAL INTRODUCTION BY

Dean L. May

University of Utah Press
Salt Lake City

Utah Pioneer Sesquicentennial
Celebration Coordinating Council

Design by Joanne Poon
Composition by Typeworks
Separations by Interwest Graphics
Printed by Sung In Printing
Printed in Republic of Korea

LIBRARY OF CONGRESS CATALOGING-IN-PUBLICATION DATA

Covington, Kae, 1952–
    Gathered in time : Utah quilts and their makers, settlement to 1950 /
Kae Covington ; with a historical introduction by Dean L. May.
       p.   cm.
    ISBN 0-87480-541-4 (alk. paper)
    1. Quilting—Utah—History. 2. Quiltmakers—Utah—Biography. 3. Quilts—Utah—
Catalogs. I. Title.
TT835.C695   1997
746.46'092'2792—dc21   97-4034

Special thanks are given by
the Utah Quilt Heritage Board to the
George S. and Dolores Doré Eccles Foundation

GEORGE S. AND DOLORES DORÉ ECCLES

F O U N D A T I O N

What Shall the Harvest Be?

Sowing the seed by the daylight fair,
Sowing the seed by the noonday glare,
Sowing the seed by the fading light,
Sowing the seed in the solemn night,
Sowing the seed with an aching heart,
Sowing the seed while the teardrops start,

Oh, what shall the harvest be?
Sown in the darkness or sown in the light,
Sown in our weakness or sown in our might,
Gathered in time or eternity
Sure, ah, sure, will the harvest be.

Words by Mrs. Emily S. Oakey
Music by P. P. Bliss

CONTENTS

PREFACE

The quilts the early pioneers who settled in Utah brought with them were part of their normal household goods, always considered a necessity during the harsh cold of winter. There were a few families who managed to make the trip across the plains with some of their lovely linen and fine, heirloom quilts intact. They were fortunate indeed. Where it was possible, these fine quilts were spared heavy use and reserved for the best beds.

For some families, having reached the Salt Lake Valley was not the end of their journey. They sometimes were "called" by leaders of the Church of Jesus Christ of Latter-day Saints to go and settle in remote areas beyond the valley. The geography of Utah, being what it is, meant that some families settled in isolated areas where travel was difficult at best and nearly impossible in winter. Quilts, along with animal hides, were used as protection against the bitter cold for traveling in wagons or buggies.

The names of men are those most often recorded in history, but the women were there all along; and the quilts they produced reveal much of the history of the time in which they lived. During those early, difficult times, many of their quilts were strictly for everyday, utilitarian needs by their large families. These quilts were crafted from worn coats and trousers or any material a woman was able to come by. Nothing was wasted. Often the lining was of feed sacks and the batting of homegrown, hand-carded wool. Frayed and worn quilts were re-covered—recycling is not a new idea.

In spite of their sometimes bleak circumstances, these pioneer women possessed an urge for artistic expression that is universal. This urge prompted these unrecognized artists with no formal training to turn quilting into a labor of love for their families. As women began to feel more settled in their frontier lives, their ideas evolved from making strictly utilitarian quilts to creating beautiful, but necessary, ones, such as those made from feed sacks that were color coordinated in the Trip Around the World pattern. Bags of fabric scraps were found in virtually every household, and many handsome quilts were created from their contents. The perennial favorite Double Wedding Ring seemed to appear everywhere. Crazy Quilts were made from precious scraps of velvet, silk, and other fine fabrics saved from Sunday-best dresses. Elegant stitches were carefully embroidered into and around the patches. This practice afforded the maker the opportunity to display her needle skills. Crazy Quilts were mostly decorative, but the many different motifs have an interesting history all their own.

Most silk patches on quilts have disintegrated by the time a quilt is a hundred years old. Colors fade and threads begin to ravel. A span of a hundred years changes most things. It was for this reason a documentation program was begun in Utah, lest the history of these wonderful quilts and the stories of their makers be forever lost.

When the Utah Quilt Guild was organized in 1977, it was unique in that it was, at the time, the only statewide quilt guild in America. The purpose of the Utah Quilt Guild was, and still is, "to encourage, promote, and preserve the art of quilt making in Utah by developing an appreciation of fine quilts; sponsoring and supporting quilting activities, teaching quilt-making techniques and knowledge of textiles and patterns; and cultivating knowledge and history of quilting and quilt makers."

A ground swell of sentiment within the Utah Quilt Guild led to a decision that something should be done to preserve the history of the quilts in Utah and record the stories of the women who made them while verification was still a possibility. For such a prodigious undertaking, the Utah Quilt Heritage Corporation was formed. Documentation Days were held from 1988 to 1994 in twenty-six different locations throughout the state. More than 2,200 quilts were documented. Willing and hardworking volunteers offered their services. No one received pay for the job done. Still there were many expenses. The cost of film for the photography alone kept eating away at a modest budget. Many kind people contributed money. A local quilt shop, Gentler Times, donated a bolt of duck to make aprons for the volunteers. These aprons were worn to protect the quilts—not the volunteers. Another local quilt shop, Quilters' Quarters, donated all of the material to make a fund-raising quilt with a theme related to the history of Utah. The motifs chosen were Tree of Life—big families are the norm in Utah; Delectable Mountains, because the Rocky Mountains traverse the state north to south; and roses. The wide border with a print containing roses denoted the promise to the weary pioneers that the desert would "blossom as the rose." Yet another quilt shop, Quilts, Etc., donated three volumes of a quilt identification book for our use. One generous member made five beautiful quilt tops that were quilted by staff members, then sold to help finance the project.

After all the documentation, there was still the formidable cost of getting the book published. Financial aid from grants and personal donations have made that possible.

The gracious ladies of Tooele accepted the invitation/challenge to host the first Documentation Day. Documentation Days have always been busy, strenuous, and long. The incoming quilts are registered and photographed and then carried to the tables where they are measured and carefully examined to determine type of fabric, thread, dyes used, lining, binding, level of proficiency of the quilter, and all other vital statistics. The only reward for the documenters is the quite wonderful gloved-hands-on experience of studying the quilts and learning their stories.

Not all who brought quilts were aware of what they had. Several lovely old quilts that had been stored for years between mattress and bedsprings carried permanent rust rings to prove it. It was easy to spot women who treasured their quilts. They carried them carefully, close to their hearts, with their arms wrapped lovingly around them. They watched with a sharp eye to see that no harm came to them, much as if each quilt were a member of the family. They stood at the side of the table while their quilts were examined and listened intently as the documentations were carried out. This project stirred many of the present-day owners of the old quilts to search their family records to glean the details of the lives of those long-ago artists in aprons who helped tackle a wilderness and tame at least a small part of the desert.

Documentation actually began before the Utah Quilt Heritage Corporation was fully incorporated, the driving force being the fear that, like patches of old silk, precious histories might fade into oblivion. The volunteers pressed forward, firm in the belief that their first priority must be to get out and find the quilts and gather the stories. The culmination of this effort by so many people finally brings a late recognition to those undaunted artists of a time gone by. The precious pictures and life stories are now collected and safely stored. The publication of this book makes a large part of that history available for all the world to see and appreciate.

Eunice Young
Past President, Utah Quilt Guild
Past President, Utah Quilt Heritage Corporation

INTRODUCTION

There are worlds of differences between the rich green meadows surrounding the thatched cottage in Aalborg, Denmark, where Celia Johanna Petersen (p. 66) and her husband, Peter Christian, began their family in the 1870s and the arid fields near Manti, Utah, where they ended their years. Their home in Denmark had a pond nearby, and they could see ships on the deep waters of the North Sea from their front door. But their life was not as easy as the land promised. Johanna was a working mother, taking wool brought home from shearing by Peter, washing and carding, spinning and weaving, to make clothes for family use and for sale.

The Petersens were converted by Mormon missionaries in the 1870s, who taught the doctrine that Latter-day Saints should gather together to prepare for last days. In 1884 they dutifully left Denmark to travel to the Mormon Zion, first Peter and their son, Hyrum; later Johanna and the two daughters, Stena and Elsa. Stena remembered that when they landed in New York, "everything looked so funny—clothes were funny, wagons were different, and people talked so funny and everything was so big and strange." We don't have her reaction on seeing the desert valley setting of Ephraim, Utah, but we do know that poverty still dogged them there and that Johanna continued to supplement the meager family income by sewing. Though poor in material goods, social life was rich in the little Mormon town, for their custom was to build houses together, where all could readily meet for church, social, and civic activities, the men commuting to farmland on the outskirts.

There was a down side to this closeness. Frequent epidemics carried by drinking water from the irrigation ditches lining the streets took a devastating toll on the lives of children. Their daughter, Elsa, died in Ephraim from diphtheria, and the family later moved to Manti, the regional capital, where they bought a house and five acres. There the couple lived out their lives in a nurturing community of Saints, never doubting, as far as we know, that they had made the right decision in choosing it over the green meadows of Denmark. And in 1918, two years before her death, Johanna created a quilt for the wedding of her granddaughter, a Wool Biscuit Quilt (p. 66), made of patch blocks, lightly stuffed with wool to give them a three-dimensional quality and stitched together with skills accrued from a lifetime of labor. It is a treasured family heirloom.

The Johanna Petersen story is a common one. With appropriate variations, the theme was repeated hundreds of times in early Utah by settlers of many backgrounds and religious persuasions, their stories remembered only by their descendants. That is why the accomplishment of the Utah Quilt Heritage Corporation in assembling this book is so important. It brings the stories of these remarkable women to a broader public, linking the art to the artists, and in so doing fills the bare lattice of history with color and substance.

Interwoven in their stories is that of the Mormon role in Utah's history and settlement. It is a story as variegated, as dramatic, as the quilts themselves. A young man in New York State had visions that led him to found a new faith. Organized in 1830, the Church of Jesus Christ of Latter-day Saints, or the Mormon church, as it came to be known, sent missionaries throughout the United States, into England, Wales,

Scotland, and Denmark, scouring the globe and bringing a harvest of converts like the Petersens home to the Mormon Zion.

The destination of these Latter-day Saints, as they called themselves, varied from time to time. Facing mounting opposition, Joseph Smith and a small band of followers fled from New York to Kirtland, Ohio, east of Cleveland, in late 1830. Quilter Elvira Pamela Mills Cox (p. 28) and her family were among the Kirtland settlers. There Smith oversaw the building of the first L.D.S. temple, while at the same time designating Independence, Missouri, now a suburb of Kansas City, as the new gathering place for converts. Those who had gathered to Missouri were met with hostility by previous settlers and in 1833 driven across the Missouri River, north and, from there, northeastward into central Missouri's Caldwell County.

The Ohio Saints in the meantime completed and dedicated their temple, amidst great outpourings of the spirit, but the failure of a bank championed by Joseph Smith caused them and those loyal to the Smiths to flee, joining the Missouri group in the fall of 1838. They arrived just in time to become embroiled in a political fracas that led to violence. Governor Boggs of Missouri ordered that the Mormons "must be exterminated or driven from the state," and a party of state militia killed eighteen Mormons at Haun's Mill, where they had taken refuge in an unchinked blacksmith shop. Quilter Jane Walker Smith (p. 56) was present at that tragedy and Sarah Ann Howard Laney's (p. 44) husband, Isaac, was wounded in the shooting.

Forced to flee again, the refugees headed east, across the Mississippi, where citizens of Quincy, Illinois, provided succor. Shortly thereafter they relocated on a swampy tract of land upriver, calling their new city Nauvoo. Quilter Elizabeth Terry Heward (p. 6) traveled to Nauvoo from Canada to visit her parents in 1842 and the next year, after her husband's death, returned to start a new life for herself among the people she had long wished to join. She remained in the city, watching it burgeon as new converts from the British Isles began to pour into this most recent of the Saints' gathering places. It was there that the Relief Society, the Mormon women's organization, was founded in 1842, an event attended by quilter Martha McBride Knight (p. 42). Martha Knight and Elizabeth Heward no doubt remembered the terrible day in 1844 when Joseph Smith and his brother Hyrum were killed. They knit and sewed clothing for the men hastening completion of their temple as Brigham Young assumed leadership, and were among those forced to abandon Nauvoo and the newly completed temple beginning in February 1846.

The trek across Iowa that spring and summer was a trial and a misery. The federal government provided relief as it could, recruiting some five hundred men and some of their wives as laundresses to join a march to the West as part of the Mexican War. Eunice Reasor Brown (p. 2) was a laundress for the Mormon Battalion, eventually making it to Utah with a striking blue and white woven coverlet, a Double Nine Patch quilt, and precious little else. The expedition provided cash and clothing for the Mormons, but left the Martha Knights and Elizabeth Hewards in the hastily built log village on the Missouri known as Winter Quarters, short on the brawn needed to continue their journey west. Their winter there was bitter and pestilential, but in April an advance party set out for the Rocky Mounatins, and in late July entered the Salt Lake Valley, which Brigham Young declared would be the new gathering place for his followers. Mormons from America, Europe, and the British Isles began immediately to flow, as writer William Mulder put it, "homeward to Zion."

Some families remained along the Missouri until 1852, moving east across the river to Kanesville, named in honor of Col. Thomas L. Kane, a friend and advocate of the refugees. Martha Knight and her family left there in 1850. Her narrative does not mention which traveling "company" she came with, though she could have told us. The companies were organized into groups of ten, fifty, and a hundred wagons, with a captain over each, the whole company taking the name of the appointed leader. Quilter Eveline Allen Cottam (p. 18) remembered traveling overland with the George A. Smith Company, arriving in late October of 1849. Between 1856 and 1860, some 3,000 Mormons walked across Nebraska and Wyoming to Utah, pulling a few possessions in two-wheeled handcarts, among them Julia Ann Collett Cantwell (p. 34).

Salt Lake City was in some sense the western Ellis Island of Mormon immigrants. Upon arriving they were greeted and cared for, then began to disperse to colonies being established further and further from the Salt Lake Valley. Soon, there were colonies south to Las Vegas and San Bernardino, north to eastern Idaho and western Wyoming, and by the 1880s to Chihuahua and Sonora, Mexico, and Alberta, Canada. When a new settlement was needed, those already established were often "called" by church leaders to provide individuals with needed skills and leadership. In 1865 Elvira Pamela Mills

Cox's husband (p. 28) was called to help found new colonies along the Muddy River in what is now Nevada. Some five hundred settlements were made by Latter-day Saints in this pattern continuing up through the end of the nineteenth century. The lives of our quilters seem often an unending round of "calls" and "missions," suggesting a level of communal commitment rare in our time.

Men were called on proselytizing missions as well, leaving wives to support themselves and families and to try to gain a surplus to send to their husbands. Ella Hammond Campbell (p. 96) was left alone with two children and later with eight when her husband was called on missions to England and the northern United States. The Mormon practice of polygamous marriage further complicated the lives of many, with some husbands dividing time between two or more wives and families. Ruth Ridge Moses (p. 32) was a second wife of Julian Moses. Mary Roskelley (p. 98) was one of five wives of Samuel Roskelley. With minimal medical facilities, death from disease and accident were common as well. Sarah Elizabeth Crook Carlile (p. 58) was widowed with eight children, an all too common experience. Thus, these women learned to be unusually independent and resourceful. Those qualities show in their craft, many of the quilts clearly pieced together from bits of fabric left over from the making of clothing or with usable patches gleaned from worn clothes.

Collectively, our quilters endured the rigors of pioneering a new land, and were a part of all the triumphs and adventures of that enterprise. Some, such as Elizabeth Jackson Reid (p. 50), kept house at first in dugouts or wagon beds. Danish-born Karen Marie Nielsen

Toft Johnson (p. 20) no doubt wept as promising fields were decimated by hordes of locusts, then marveled as seagulls descended to gorge themselves on the insects, saving part of the crop. Some, including Ann Etta Eckersley Draper (p. 12), fled from their homes during the Utah War of 1857 when federal troops under Albert Sidney Johnston were sent to put down a reported rebellion among the Mormons. Jane Walker Smith (p. 56) cheerfully tended malodorous silkworms as part of an ongoing effort to develop home industries.

Women like Mary Ann Ford Simmons (p. 40), born to wealth and privilege, found themselves reduced to the most humble of circumstances. Mary was a well-educated, polished English girl, and founder of her own children's school, until her conversion to Mormonism. In Utah she gathered sego lily bulbs for sustenance, and mothered her children in a log cabin with dirt floor and roof where "when it had quit raining outside, it would still be raining inside." At Brigham Young's urging, women, such as Inez Heaton Hoyt (p. 104), participated in the 1870s in forming communal "United Orders" throughout Mormon country to lessen dependence on the outside world, promote simplicity, and build a sense of cooperation and togetherness in their economic life as in their spiritual and social lives.

From the beginning, quilters of many faiths made Utah their home and contributed to the tradition. The Rebekah Lodges of Utah are represented in a Friendship/Album quilt (p. 124), and Mayme Pargis (p. 118) of Lynndyl stiched an exquisite Rose Star quilt during the war years. The efforts of all these Utahns left a tradition of communal and cooperative

labor sorely needed in our time and perpetuated still among those women (and a few men) who continue to gather around quilting frames and, while sharing their dreams and their fears, combine their stitches to produce a single object of enduring beauty.

And thus, the story continues into our century and, thanks to the work of the Utah Quilt Heritage Corporation, will be carried to the next. Jeana Kimball saw clearly that "each quilt, step by step, speaks for its maker—her voice is clearly there, between the fabric and lines of stitches." Of course she is exactly right. One cannot look at Johanna Petersen's quilt without wanting to touch it and thus connect with this remarkable woman and her strong spirit. Being gathered in time, the strands of these quilters' lives, like their quilts, bespeak not only the makers but also the times from which they came. Theirs is indeed a legacy to be reckoned with.

Dean L. May

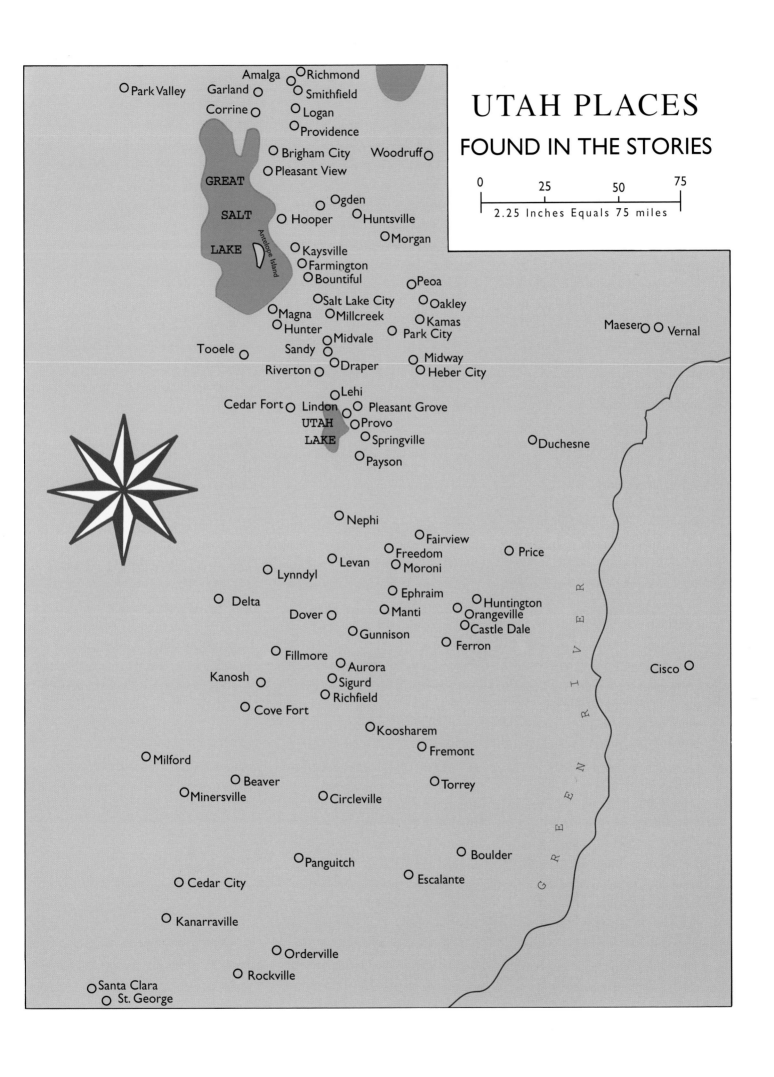

UTAH PLACES
FOUND IN THE STORIES

0   25   50   75

2.25 Inches Equals 75 miles

Park Valley

Amalga   ○ Richmond
Garland ○   ○ Smithfield
Corrine ○   ○ Logan
   ○ Providence
○ Brigham City   Woodruff ○
○ Pleasant View

GREAT

SALT

LAKE

○ Ogden
○ Hooper   ○ Huntsville
○ Morgan

Antelope Island

○ Kaysville
○ Farmington
○ Bountiful
   ○ Peoa
○ Salt Lake City   ○ Oakley
Magna ○   ○ Millcreek   ○ Kamas
Hunter ○   ○ Park City
   ○ Midvale
Tooele ○   Sandy ○   ○ Midway
Riverton ○   ○ Draper   ○ Heber City

Maesero ○ ○ Vernal

○ Lehi
Cedar Fort ○   Lindon ○ ○ Pleasant Grove
UTAH   ○ Provo
LAKE   ○ Springville
   ○ Payson

○ Duchesne

○ Nephi
   ○ Fairview
   ○ Freedom   ○ Price
○ Levan   ○ Moroni

Lynndyl ○

○ Delta   ○ Ephraim
Dover ○   ○ Manti   ○ Huntington
   ○ Orangeville
○ Gunnison   ○ Castle Dale
   ○ Ferron

○ Fillmore
   ○ Aurora
Kanosh ○   ○ Sigurd
   ○ Richfield
○ Cove Fort

Cisco ○

G R E E N   R I V E R

○ Koosharem
   ○ Fremont
○ Milford
○ Beaver   ○ Torrey
○ Minersville
○ Circleville

○ Boulder
○ Panguitch
○ Escalante
○ Cedar City

○ Kanarraville

○ Orderville
○ Rockville
○ Santa Clara
○ St. George

Eunice Reasor Brown

Knowing that she would soon be traveling into unsettled territory where supplies could not be casually purchased whenever needed, Eunice Reasor Brown prepared herself. She made sure that her four children and her husband would be adequately clothed and that the family would have more than enough flour, salt, lard, sugar, and pork to keep them alive. She even made nine new dresses for herself. And she made certain there would be room in the wagon for her feather bed. Some thought it foolish of her to take such a luxury on the trail, but Eunice was tired of being chased away from her home and her possessions by cruel mobs attacking Mormon settlements. "They [the mobs] will not have my bed!" she declared. "If I can't take it, I will open it up and let the feathers fly!"

The journey Eunice was preparing for was not the journey to a safe place far away from mobs and persecutions the Brown family had hoped and prayed for. When Brigham Young, leader of the L.D.S. church, asked the U.S. government for help in finding someplace for the desperate pioneers to settle, the government responded by asking him for help in fighting the Mexican War. Under Brigham's direction, 500 men enlisted within three weeks' time, ready to make the 2,000-mile trek to California as the Mormon Battalion in exchange for a promise from the government that the Mormons could then settle on any Indian lands they chose. When James Brown enlisted, he took his mother's maiden name, "Polly," to avoid confusion with other James Browns in the Battalion.

Thereafter, he was known as "James Polly Brown."

Many of the enlisted men, including James Polly Brown, took their families on the march. Eunice signed on as a laundress for seven dollars a month, and their two oldest sons, fourteen-year-old Neuman and sixteen-year-old Robert, worked as teamsters for the Battalion. On July 20, 1846, 584 men, women, and children left Council Bluffs, Iowa, marching to the tune of "The Girl I Left Behind." Their mission was to reinforce the "Army of the West" in the war against Mexico and to build a wagon road from Santa Fe to California. The Mormon Battalion accomplished both assignments admirably.

The first ten days of the journey were 200 blurred miles of mud, mosquitoes, and violent rainstorms. Malaria was widespread, claiming the life of their commander, James Allen, in Fort Leavenworth, Kansas. Here, each man was paid a "uniform allowance" of forty-two dollars, which most of the men sent back to the families who had stayed in Iowa.

On August 12, the second leg of the journey began under the command of Lt. A. J. Smith. His only concern was in moving everyone in and associated with the Battalion the 900 miles to Santa Fe as rapidly as possible. He drove them hard and fast in the unbearable heat, and many of the soldiers and their families became ill. At the crossing of the Arkansas River in Colorado, Lieutenant Smith sent three detachments of the sick, including most of the women and children, to spend the winter in Pueblo, Colorado. Pvt. James Polly Brown was with the soldiers who went on ahead to build shelters for the 273 people who would live there

through the winter. He and his family remained with the group, offering aid and encouragement, until the War with Mexico ended in May of 1847.

Eunice and James Polly Brown arrived in the Salt Lake Valley on July 29, 1847, only five days after the arrival of the first of the emigrants, including Brigham Young. They had been delayed a few days in June while Eunice gave birth to her seventh child, John Taylor Brown. Among the few possessions that arrived in the valley with Eunice was her beautiful blue and white woven coverlet. The feather bed had been sold earlier to replace a tender-footed ox.

The Brown family remained in the Salt Lake Valley for two years, until receiving a call from L.D.S. church leaders to settle in Manti, Utah, where they arrived on November 19, 1849. Their first winter was spent in a cave dug into the hillside, a home they quickly abandoned in the spring when hundreds of rattlesnakes began crawling from their nests in the warming earth. In 1851 Eunice gave birth to her eighth child, a daughter she named after herself. When little Eunice Ann was seven years old, her mother passed away. Her husband wrote in the family Bible, "Eunice Reasor Brown my wife died July 18th, 1858, 12 o'clock 15 min." James Polly Brown was then called to settle in Rockville, Utah, leaving Eunice buried in Manti and sending the children to live with various other people.

The homespun coverlet was probably made by a traveling weaver in Indiana from wool supplied by Eunice in a pattern she had chosen. There was a fringe along the edges of the blanket, which is actually two 36-inch widths of woven fabric sewn together. Many years

later, after a visiting family went home, the owners discovered the coverlet had disappeared from the trunk where it was kept. They worried and fretted about the coverlet, but never accused anyone of taking it. About seven years later, it miraculously reappeared in the trunk when the family visited again. It was well worn and the fringe was gone, but it was otherwise intact.

1830

Woven Coverlet

84" x 66½"

Wool

Maker unknown

Owned by Ruth Davenport Scow

Sarah
Adams
Bitely
Conrad

■ ■

It is easy to imagine Sarah Conrad stepping out of time to pass on her quilt to the next generation for safekeeping. There have been six generations of owners, including the maker, and each "keeper of the quilt" has made it a sacred duty to preserve this treasure from the past. The colors are astonishing; the fabrics are in perfect condition. Sarah would be proud of her descendants and the respect and honor they have shown her.

Sarah Adams Bitely was born in Vermont State in 1802, named for the midwife who delivered her. At the age of twenty-eight she married Charles Ferdinand Conrad in Seneca, New York. In 1831, with their infant daughter Elizabeth, they moved to Michigan to homestead eighty acres of thickly timbered land populated with deer, bear, and wild panthers. The Conrad family grew to include eleven children, two of whom died as infants. Charles became prominent in local politics, serving as a justice of the peace and holding other elected offices from time to time.

Sarah joined the Church of Jesus Christ of Latter-day Saints in 1843 after listening to her son Serrine explain why he had joined. Her oldest daughter, Elizabeth, also became a member of the new religion and eventually Charles was baptized, too. Living among and joining with the Saints became Sarah's greatest desire. She and her husband left for Nauvoo, Illinois, getting as far as La Harpe, before hearing of the murders of the L.D.S. prophet, Joseph Smith, and his brother Hyrum. Charles became disenchanted with the church, commenting that it couldn't be much of a religion if it was that easy to kill the leader.

Sarah and Charles eventually separated, and in 1862, with her children now grown, Sarah packed her Lady of the Lake quilt and, together with another single woman, made the journey to Utah. She settled in Provo where some of her children already had homes. Her daughter Elizabeth traveled to Utah with her four children in 1870 to join her husband, James Hooks, who had been working on the railroad. Sarah lived in a little log cabin near Elizabeth and her family until she could no longer take care of herself. She died in Elizabeth's home in 1879 at the age of seventy-seven.

Sarah's lovely hand-pieced quilt evokes memories of a warm summer's day spent sailing or watching boats sail out to sea. The tiny triangles used in the sashing and border are like miniature sailboats moving gracefully to and fro on the surface of the water, their sails filled with an ocean breeze. The entire quilt is stitched with white cotton thread in a diagonal, allover grid with seven to eight very even stitches to the inch. A narrow, homemade binding finishes the edges.

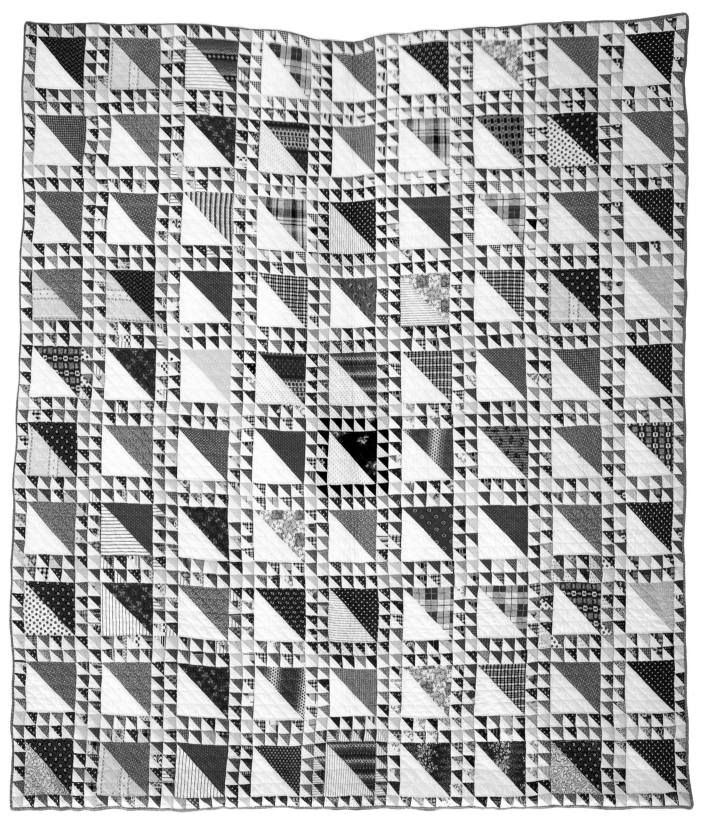

1830–1835

Lady of the Lake

76" x 86"

Cotton

Made by Sarah Adams Bitely Conrad

(1802–1879)

Made in New York or Michigan

Owned by LaMar and Marian Ercanbrack

Elizabeth
Terry
Heward

Elizabeth Terry Heward lived two very different lives in the course of her sixty-four years on earth: the first as the lonely wife of an often drunk and abusive innkeeper, the other as the valued companion of an honest, hardworking farmer and a loving mother to their four sons and four daughters. In her deeply personal autobiography written in 1860 "for the benefit of my children," Elizabeth describes a life of undeniable hardship, persecution, and physical and mental suffering transcended by hope, gratitude, creativity, and strength.

Elizabeth Terry was born on November 17, 1814, one of thirteen children of Parshall and Hannah Terry of Palmyra, New York. When Elizabeth was four, the family moved to upper Canada near Little York, which is now Toronto. In 1822, the Terrys settled in Albion, Canada, a land so heavily timbered there was no prairie for hundreds of miles.

In July 1833, acting on the advice of her father, Elizabeth married a young Englishman named Francis Kirby. Kirby spent most of his time drinking, playing cards, attending horse races, and singing profane songs while Elizabeth ran his tavern and cooked for the guests. After three years of marriage, Elizabeth became depressed and discouraged, spending "many hours in weeping and deep sorrow." To ease the pain and loneliness, she began writing in a journal, a practice she continued until her death.

In 1837, Elizabeth heard that Mormon preachers were some twenty miles away. She persuaded Kirby to allow them to hold a meeting in their home. Elizabeth longed to join the L.D.S. church as her parents had, but Kirby fought to keep her from them. A year later, when Elizabeth's parents were ready to sail to Far West, Missouri, to join the Saints, Kirby relented and allowed his wife to be baptized.

Elizabeth traveled to Nauvoo, Illinois, in July 1842 to see her family. Leaving Kirby was difficult and she wept openly. She wrote an affectionate letter to him, which he carried around for days, asking anyone he met to read it to him, muttering that Elizabeth was "the best woman he ever saw." When Elizabeth returned to Canada on September 20, she found her husband had died on August 31 and been buried soon after.

Bill collectors began demanding payment for Kirby's debts. In 1843, Elizabeth visited her parents in Nauvoo and tried to find employment and housing there. She encountered John Heward, a man who had once worked for Kirby in Canada and whom Elizabeth had described earlier in her journal as "a steady sober man." Aware of her circumstances, John offered to sell his farm in Belvidere, Illinois, and buy a home for her in Nauvoo. The two were married in May 1844.

After a difficult delivery, Elizabeth's first child, Rachel, was born in December 1845. In the early morning hours three months later, Rachel died. Alone, Elizabeth was so distraught she wrapped her baby in a blanket and walked to her mother's house to see if the child really was dead. They buried her on the prairie three miles east of the Nauvoo L.D.S. Temple.

In 1846, the Hewards traveled to Council Bluffs, Iowa, where they lived in a cave dug into the bank of Mosquito Creek. The dirt floors and walls were cold and damp, but Elizabeth worked to make it a home, even bearing her second child there. After almost two years, the family headed for Salt Lake in May 1848.

The trek was a difficult one for Elizabeth, who had not regained her health following her daughter Sarah's birth in March. Five months of travel brought the little family to their new home. In 1849 Elizabeth moved into a new adobe house, where she established a school, instructing children on the humane and tolerant treatment of others and the importance of obedience to their parents. Her school was well attended, with an annual program for the parents. One year, she gave each of her students a small painting she had made. She had used this talent many years earlier to embellish her unique quilt—now so threadbare and tattered—with each center square containing an individual, hand-painted leaf.

Six more children were born to the Hewards in Salt Lake City. Elizabeth continued to sew and paint and knit to add to the family income. She wrote of selling her paintings to buy thread, salt, cheese, fish, cotton cloth, and a basket. In 1858 the family settled in Draperville (now Draper, Utah), where Elizabeth lived until her death in 1878. Her descendants treasure the now-fragile quilt as a symbol of her will and stamina, traits that extend through the generations.

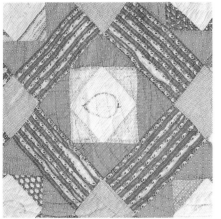

Before 1850

Square in a Square

79″ x 75″

Cotton

Made by Elizabeth Terry Heward

(1814–1878)

Probably made in Nauvoo, Hancock

County, Illinois

Owned by Evelyn Mecham Lucas

Great-grandmother Betenson's eight leather-bound trunks were a treasure cache, a secret garden to young Lu Deanne Burton. There was a trunk filled with linens, one heaped with old dishes, another with carefully folded and apparently ancient clothing. Some held pictures and the old family Bible from England. And in one there was the quilt—soft, shimmering, and mysterious. It was made in the familiar Log Cabin pattern, but the three-inch blocks with strips of silk and centers of black velvet made it look like no other quilt the young girl had ever seen. When seen from a distance, expanding black diamonds moved outward and lighter silken bands zigzagged like tiles on an exotic temple floor. The startlingly simple back of the quilt was made of plain rose-colored cotton, stitched with small yarn pompons at regular intervals. Lu Deanne inherited the quilt from her mother in 1990. For eighty-three years it had remained in the trunk, removed only as a curiosity or to get at important papers and newspaper clippings. It is now a treasure freely displayed and honored as a reminder of the strong and talented woman who made it so long ago.

Elizabeth Blanks Pengelly was born in St. Germans, England, on April 15, 1828. Nothing is known about her schooling, but she was apparently well educated and she wrote poetry. She loved art and was concerned about social matters and had very proper English manners. Her mother taught her to sew at a young age, and she became an expert seamstress, well known for her beautiful handwork.

In 1848 Elizabeth married Joseph Nathaniel Betenson, a member of the Royal Navy, the son and grandson of naval officers. They lived for five years in Devonport, leaving in 1853 for New Orleans, Louisiana, on the ship *International*. Both Elizabeth and Joseph had joined the L.D.S. church in England and longed to live among like-minded believers. They set out from New Orleans for the Salt Lake Valley in September 1853 with the C. Spencer Company of emigrants, settling in Salt Lake City for two years.

In 1855, Elizabeth's husband was called by church leaders to settle in Beaver, Utah, and Elizabeth and their baby son, Joseph Arthur, went with him. This move was a difficult one for Elizabeth. The flat, treeless countryside was in sharp contrast to the green hills and coastal vistas of her native England. There were no theaters, no libraries, no museums, and no schools. It seemed a desolate place, one she thought would be her prison, but she accepted the challenge, raising five daughters and one son, all with impeccable manners, a proper education, and a strong sense of right and wrong.

Elizabeth was an individual who was unafraid to make her opinions known. A favorite family story tells of her forthrightness when her husband was asked by local church officials to take another wife. She told Joseph that she was content as things were, to clean the house and cook the meals, but the minute he brought another wife in through the front door, she and the children would go out the back door. The subject was not mentioned again.

Elizabeth Betenson died a few months before her eightieth birthday, on February 15, 1907, in Nephi, Utah. A letter she had written shortly before her death was found among her keepsakes telling her children that they should "club together" to buy a nice coffin for her. She didn't want to be buried in "cheap flannel and wood with knotholes." She wasn't.

Elizabeth
Blanks
Pengelly
Betenson

About 1850

**Log Cabin,
Barn Raising Setting**

60″ x 66″

Silk, velvet, and cotton

Made by Elizabeth Blanks Pengelly

Betenson (1828–1907)

Probably made in Devonport, England

Owned by Lu Deanne Fischer

Matilda
Robison
King

Matilda and Thomas King arrived in Utah in 1851 with the Vincent Shurtliff Company of emigrants. The New England couple had joined the L.D.S. church in 1840, moving to Montrose, Iowa, just across the river from Nauvoo, Illinois. In 1846, they joined the exodus from Nauvoo and settled in Winter Quarters, a log-cabin village hastily constructed for Mormon emigrants that was located on the west bank of the Missouri River. Later, they moved to Missouri, where they prepared for the long, uncertain journey to the valley of the Great Salt Lake. Having arrived in Utah, they eventually settled in Millard County, living there for the next twenty-five years.

Thomas and Matilda moved their family into Cove Fort during the closing months of the Black Hawk War. Cove Fort in Millard County is a grand, square structure with lava rock walls, eighteen feet high, that run a hundred feet in each direction. An earlier fort, Fort Willden, had been abandoned on the site in 1865, leaving no protection from either Indians or severe weather conditions for travelers, U.S. mail carriers, telegraph operators, freighters, and stagecoach agents as they journeyed over the high mountain pass between Fillmore and Beaver. In 1867, Brigham Young directed Ira Hinckley to oversee the construction of the new building, which took seven months to complete. A number of families lived in the fort from time to time. The King family probably occupied the fort for only a short time, since the war came to an end in late 1867.

In the fall of 1875, the family bought land in Circle Valley in Piute County. Thomas and Matilda and some of their children moved to their Circle Valley property in 1876, where they lived the United Order with several other families. The United Order of Enoch was a communal system in which all possessions were consecrated to the L.D.S. church in exchange for a "stewardship" over a home and the resources needed to work in a chosen trade. The order had been tried by the early church membership in the 1830s, dissolving when members of the church were driven from Jackson County, Missouri, in 1833. Brigham Young's attempt to revive the system began in 1874 and spread through every community in Utah with varying degrees of success. The practice was discontinued in 1883.

Matilda brought her stately Washington's Plume quilt with her as she moved from New York to Illinois, Missouri, and finally Utah. It is a variation of the Princess Feather pattern combined with a colonial-style rose design and a broad, scalloped border.

It was during the Documentation Day that Gayle Frandsen, one of the documenters, made her own discovery: the quilt had been made by her great-grandmother! Gayle had been unaware of the quilt's existence. A quilter herself, Gayle is making a copy of this beautiful old quilt.

Before 1851

Washington's Plume

64″ x 83″

Cotton

Made by Matilda Robison King

(1811–1894)

Made in New York State

Owned by Fillmore Museum

Ann
Etta
Eckersley
Draper

There were few places Ann Etta Draper went without a needle, thread, and thimble in her pocket, whether it was to visit with a neighbor, deliver a baby, or care for the sick or dying. No doubt she even carried those items with her on the ship *The Palmyra* when she sailed from England to America with her parents, William and Hannah Eckersley, and three younger sisters in 1845. Eleven years old and newly converted to the L.D.S. church, she had a six-week voyage to busy herself with needlework and dreams of a new home with the Saints in Nauvoo, Illinois.

Life in America began badly for the Eckersley family. Ann's newborn brother died in 1846 and her father was dead a year later. Her mother found employment at The Planter's, the largest hotel in Saint Louis, and earned enough money to move the family to Council Point, Iowa. There Hannah met and married John Crompton and the family prepared for their long-awaited trip to Utah. Ann was nineteen in the spring of 1853 when they left with an independent company led by Edward Pugh, reaching Salt Lake in September.

Food was scarce and prices were high when Ann arrived in Utah. The family avoided starvation during that first winter by digging potatoes left from the fall harvest. They moved to Little Cottonwood in 1854. Ann soon found work with a prosperous family in Draper. During the Christmas holidays, her employer gave her a pan of white flour as a gift, and she walked six miles to make a present of it to her mother, who promptly made the best dinner the family had eaten since crossing the plains.

At the age of twenty-three, Ann met William Lathrop "Doc" Draper. He was several years younger than Ann and pursued her relentlessly. They married in 1857 in the city of Draper, which Doc's father had founded. Before their first year of marriage had passed, the pioneers began to abandon the Salt Lake Valley. Johnston's Army was approaching from the east, sent by the U.S. government to destroy the Mormons, or so they feared. Ann and Doc moved to Spanish Fork, then returned to Salt Lake in 1858 after an understanding with the army was reached.

In 1863 the Draper family received a call from church leaders to travel with three other families to southern Utah, where they settled Rockville. They spent five years pioneering the rugged land, leaving when Doc's health began to suffer. They returned to central Utah to live, but discovered that most of the available land and water had been claimed by older, more established settlers. So they did what they had done once before: they established a new town, named Freedom, five miles from Moroni in Sanpete County. Here they lived for the rest of their lives.

Pioneer life demanded much of Ann and she responded energetically. She bore ten children, six of whom lived to adulthood. She worked in the fields and orchards and she milked cows. She carded, spun, and wove wool into fabric for her masterful sewing projects. She was an expert at making men's trousers, and she designed original patterns for eyelet embroidery. She hand stitched beautiful dresses for her daughters and taught sewing classes in Moroni and Freedom. Ann was also the local doctor and midwife, delivering babies, administering to the sick, and preparing the dead for burial. She charged fifty

cents to a dollar to care for a mother and her new baby for three weeks; there was no charge for a needy family. And, of course, her needle, thread, and thimble went with her everywhere.

Ann had a beautiful singing voice and was an accomplished step dancer. She loved performing her fancy steps to countless encores. Her final performance took place at a Black Hawk encampment in Ephraim, where she danced before a crowd of hundreds. She had fallen and injured herself on the way to the program, but, not realizing the extent of her injuries, she had danced as enthusiastically as ever. A slow paralysis developed in her legs, and she spent the remainder of her life in a wheelchair. With Ann's generous and energetic spirit, it is unlikely the wheelchair stayed in one place for very long. She died in Freedom on the evening of June 10, 1915.

Ann's charming quilt is like a square dance viewed from above. Nine perfect squares await the fiddler to begin. It is easy to envision the tulips performing an energetic do-si-do in and out of the squares or doing the fancy step dancing Ann loved, spinning effortlessly in a scrapbag calico jig.

1855–1860

Pinwheel Star

76½″ x 88″

Cotton

Made by Ann Etta Eckersley Draper

(1834–1915)

Made in Draper, Salt Lake County, Utah

Owned by Wanda L. Bond

Fanny
Jane
Perris
Jennings

Fanny Jane Jennings has been described by one of her granddaughters as a "peppery little bundle of lively humanity. I'd say she weighed about seventy pounds, every inch alive and on the go. . . . [There was] no chronic inertia around Grandma."

Fanny Jane Perris began her life of pioneering in Gloucester, England, on October 3, 1842, a daughter of Thomas and Hannah Rebecca Spiller Perris. She was six years old in early 1849 when her family sailed to Australia. California was not the only spot in the world that year with "gold fever." Fanny's father became very wealthy from his gold diggings, and the family remained in Australia for four years.

In April 1853 Fanny set sail for California with her mother and a brother and sister. Thomas Perris remained behind to dispose of his furniture store and other holdings, planning to join his family within the year. Tragically, he lost track of his wife and children and returned to England, where he died a brokenhearted man. Meanwhile, Hannah Rebecca, wrongly informed of his death in Australia in 1854, moved on with her life, assuming herself to be a widow. She settled in San Bernardino, where the family remained until 1857. When the Mormon settlers of the area were called back to Utah, the Perris family journeyed with them.

Fanny Jane was now fifteen years old, the same age her mother had been when she married Thomas Perris. On the trip to Utah, Fanny Jane met Mansfield C. Jennings and the two were married in Las Vegas, Nevada, then a Mormon settlement, on December 29, 1857. The newlyweds settled in Beaver, Utah, while the rest of their family went on to Salt Lake City. Mansfield made his living running freight between Beaver and California. In the summer, the two went back to California, where their first child, Mary Frances, was born in December 1858. Hannah Rebecca joined them there to help during the birth of her first grandchild.

Sometime in 1857 or 1858, Fanny Jane and her mother received a copy of a San Bernardino newspaper containing a notice addressed to the heirs of Thomas Perris. His sizeable fortune had fallen into the hands of the Chancery Court in England, which was searching for his heirs. Mansfield immediately sold his livestock and property and sailed with his wife and daughter to England, where Fanny hoped to claim her family's share of the property. For two years they remained in England trying to settle the matter. Their biggest obstacle was their marriage, of which they seemed unable to provide proof, at least proof that would satisfy the English courts. Eventually, they had to be married again before Fanny Jane could claim what was rightfully hers. In the end, she received only half of the fortune, the other half collectable only upon her death.

The couple returned to America with their daughter and a new baby, Sarah Annette, who had been born in 1860. They landed in New York and began planning their trip to Utah. Mansfield bought two teams of oxen and two wagons, which they loaded with the necessary supplies and household goods. Included were a new cookstove bought in New York and a fine set of white china dishes Fanny Jane had purchased in England. Fanny drove one team of oxen, with her babies in the back of the wagon, and Mansfield drove the other.

The journey went well until one afternoon when the oxen bolted, nearly causing the death of Fanny Jane and her children. The company had traveled a great distance that day and the animals had been without water since early morning. When the oxen saw a large stream of water ahead, they rushed into it, somehow pulling the wagon box from the wagon. As Fanny and her daughters floated down the deep, swift stream, their terrified screams attracted some men downstream who were able to pull the box ashore. Repairs were made and the trip continued. Verda Hicken, Fanny's great-granddaughter, owns a small china closet, a small round table, and a beaded cape that probably floated down the river in the wagon box with Fanny.

Fanny Jane and Mansfield settled in Springville, Utah, on the edge of Hobble Creek, a picturesque stream surrounded by tall willows. Fanny and her beautiful china dishes became well known: she generously shared them with the town for such special occasions as weddings and dinners for visiting church authorities. She gave birth to two more children in Springville, Mansfield Frederick in 1863 and Joannah Eliza in 1866.

In 1869 the family was called by church leaders to help settle the town of Levan in Juab County. Mansfield traveled there first, where he built a large one-room cabin for his family. He returned to Springville to dispose of his property and prepare for the family's trip. It was December when they finally left for their new home. The bitter cold nearly froze the family to death. Imagine their joy and gratitude to find a fire blazing in their new fireplace, a never-to-be-forgotten welcome from neighbors.

After nearly thirteen years of marriage, Fanny Jane and Mansfield divorced because of "lack of support." Twenty years later, Fanny Jane married James Wilson, the postmaster of Levan. They remained in Levan for the duration of their twenty-nine–year marriage. James died in April 1919, and Fanny died the following September. The death of "Grandma Wilson," the little dynamo of a woman who always wore a white collar and had every hair in place, was greatly mourned by the residents of the town.

1860

Tumblers

78" x 66½"

Cotton

Made by Fanny Jane Perris Jennings
Wilson (1842–1919)
Made in Levan, Juab County, Utah
Owned by Verda Hicken

Elizabeth
McKay
Treseder

The British isle of Jersey sits a mere twelve miles off the coast of France. It is a tiny island, measuring ten miles, east to west, and five miles, north to south, with deep valleys and 400-foot cliffs lined with caves. People have lived on the island since pre-historic times, and it was known to the Romans as Caesarea. French land-owners dominated the island until 1204, and most of the current inhabitants descend from them. The economy is based on vegetables, fruits, and flowers grown for the British market and on the export of Jersey cattle, the only breed allowed on the island since 1789.

It was to this tranquil, fragrant island that Elizabeth and Richard Treseder and their two sons came sometime between 1838 and 1840. Elizabeth was born in Ireland, although her father was from Scotland and her mother was English. Thomas McKay, her father, was a ship builder and the family lived wherever ships were being built. Richard Treseder's father was also a ship builder, but Richard chose to be a tailor like his uncle. The couple were married in Devonshire, England, on November 14, 1833.

Elizabeth's first three children—all sons—were born in England. Richard, the second son, died at six months of age. Ten more children were born to the Treseders on Jersey; four were buried there before the family left the island for America in 1855. The year of 1853 must have been especially difficult for Elizabeth. Her eleven-year-old daughter, Emma, died in March and, less than a month later, eight-month-old Emily was gone. In early November, she gave birth to her last child, a son named Francis McKay.

Elizabeth and Richard joined the L.D.S. church in 1847 and immediately began planning for their emigration to Zion (the Mormons' religious designation for the place they believed would become the permanent home for the Saints). On March 29, 1855, the family boarded a ship and, with 431 other Mormons, set sail for America on April 17. After five weeks at sea, they arrived in Philadelphia, Pennsylvania. Here the family remained for a year while Richard worked at odd jobs to earn money for the journey west to Utah. The family also lived in Pittsburgh and New York for six more years, never losing sight of their dream to live in Deseret (the early name of the Mormons' Utah homeland). The three oldest sons were sent ahead to prepare for the family's arrival in Salt Lake, which finally took place in September 1862. Richard was able to establish a tailor shop on Main Street between First and Second South streets, a small shop where he would sit cross-legged in one of the windows to sew his hand-tailored suits.

Elizabeth never returned to her Jersey island home, but her Flower Basket quilt must have transported her there in her thoughts and in her heart. There is a youthful quality of cele-bration about it. Baskets filled with flowers of every imaginable variety peek out from behind the red lattice sashing crisscrossed like the stone paths in an English garden. How it must have comforted her to imagine the flowers being picked and brought to her by the children she had lost so long ago. And how it must have cheered her to remember the gardens of Jersey where the pansies and the roses and the bleeding hearts seemed to grow without effort in the mild climate. Her wool fabrics and crewel embroidery stir memories of sunshine and soft petals and spring. It tells Jean Christensen everything she needs to know about her great-grandmother Elizabeth.

1861

Flower Baskets

72" x 73"

Cotton, wool

Made by Elizabeth McKay Treseder

(1811–1891)

Made in England and New York, USA

Owned by Jean Christensen

Eveline

Allen

Cottam

■ ■

If you look closely at this quilt stitched in 1866 by seventeen-year-old Eveline Allen, you can see three-dimensional blocks tumbling from the rolling stars at the center of each square. Eight blocks with shared sides and tops are difficult to view for any length of time without experiencing a whirling sensation. The diagonal set of the squares and the cable-stitch quilting only add to the feeling as the calico stars appear to spin into the blue-topped cubes.

Eveline Allen was born in 1849 to Philo Allen and Lucy Alvord Hawks in Council Bluffs, Iowa, which the Mormons had reached in 1846 after fleeing Nauvoo, Illinois. At the time of Eveline's birth, Council Bluffs was known as Kanesville, renamed by Brigham Young in 1848 in honor of Colonel Thomas Kane, who had helped the Mormons in their migrations. The Allens crossed the plains with the George A. Smith Company of emigrants, reaching the Salt Lake Valley on October 27, 1849. Eveline was nine months old.

Salt Lake City was Eveline's home until 1867, when she married William Cottam, a native Englishman who had immigrated to Nauvoo, Illinois, with his parents when he was a year old and traveled to Utah in 1851 or 1852. The couple lived briefly in Weber and Rich counties until returning to Salt Lake for the birth of their third child in 1872.

In November 1877, Eveline and William moved to Escalante in south-central Utah. Escalante had originally been named Potato Valley for the edible wild potatoes found there by members of a Mormon cavalry unit that happened onto the valley while pursuing Indians during the Black Hawk War in 1866. In 1875, at the suggestion of A. H. Thompson, who was a member of the John Wesley Powell Colorado River expedition, four pioneer settlers from Panguitch changed the name to Escalante to honor the Spanish explorer Father Silvestre Vélez de Escalante. It is possible that the Cottam family settled there because Eveline's parents already lived there; the first log cabin in the area was built by Philo Allen.

Eveline took her treasured Rolling Star quilt to Escalante, rolled up in a clean flour sack. She thought of the quilt as a memory or friendship quilt because her family, friends, and neighbors had joined in the quilting of it. Some of the tiny, even stitches visible on the quilt were made by one of her dearest friends who later became a wife of Brigham Young. The quilt was only brought out for special occasions. Her instructions to her posterity were that the quilt be prized, kept in the family, and handed down to the oldest female in each generation.

Nine children were born to Eveline and William Cottam. Eveline outlived her husband by two decades, dying in Escalante at the age of eighty-five.

1866

Rolling Star

76″ x 88½″

Cotton

Made by Eveline Allen Cottam

(1849–1934)

Made in Salt Lake City, Salt Lake County,

Utah

Owned by Lasca Osborn Eyre

Karen

Marie

Nielsen

Toft

Johnson

Karen Johnson left Denmark in December 1853 with everything she valued: her husband, her four children, a few necessary possessions, and her faith. The Johnson family was headed for Utah, gathering with other Scandinavian immigrants to live in their "Zion" with other Latter-day Saints. But during the crossing of the North Sea to Liverpool, England, she lost nearly everything that mattered. When she disembarked in January, she carried the tiny body of one of her children; her husband, John Peter, carried another. Silently, they handed them to members of the L.D.S. church in England, leaving them to be buried in Liverpool, surrendering them to the wintry ground of an alien land. Then Karen and her husband boarded the *Benjamin Adam* and sailed to America.

The seven-week journey was long and lonely for Karen. In March 1854 the ship docked in New Orleans, leaving the Johnsons and their comrades halfway to their Promised Land. They spent the spring months procuring a covered wagon, a team of oxen, and supplies for the westward trek. They joined the Andrew Larson Company and reached Utah without incident in October, ten months after leaving Denmark. Karen was seven months pregnant.

For the Johnsons, on entering the Salt Lake Valley, it might have seemed like one more disaster in a long line of tragedies that had pursued them since their departure from Denmark, for the Saints had endured another of many locust attacks on their grainfields. The voracious insects had devoured everything, forcing the people to subsist on boiled grass and greens for their first year. These locusts were Rocky Mountain crickets, later known as "Mormon crickets." As long as a man's thumb, they seemed impossible to exterminate. The crickets had first plagued the pioneers in the spring of 1848, swarming in hordes upon the newly planted crops. All attempts to destroy them by fire, beating, and drowning were in vain. At last, flocks of seagulls descended as if from the heavens to gorge themselves on the crickets, saving the valuable crops.

John found work as a builder and contractor in Provo, thirty miles south of Salt Lake. After the birth of their fifth child, Rebecca, he walked from Provo to Salt Lake on weekends to be with his family. In 1856, they moved permanently to Provo, where they lived the rest of their lives. Five more children were born to them. Karen's home was the tallest house in Provo, a three-story beauty built by John. The home was always open to arriving Scandinavian immigrants in need of food or shelter.

Karen's coverlet is an exquisite garden of scrapbag hexagons. There are pastels, plaids, and tiny floral prints. The red pieces that frame the central medallion are striped with white, the stripes on each piece matching perfectly where they are hand stitched together. There is no quilting or batting. The spread was originally made in 1870 as a lightweight coverlet for a grandson's small, walnut youth bed. The bed is still being used by a great-great-great-grandson in Beaver, Utah.

1870

Flower Garden

53″ x 78″

Cotton

Made by Karen Marie Nielsen Toft
Johnson (1825–1890)

Made in Provo, Utah County, Utah

Owned by Anne Swindlehurst

Celestia
Melissa
Terry
Petersen

Sarah
Vail
Terry

■ ■

A larger-than-life statue of an elderly couple sits in the Museum of History and Art in the little Utah town of Fairview. Created by sculptor Avard Fairbanks and entitled "Love and Devotion," it is a tribute to marriage, a portrait of a couple wedded for eighty-two years. The husband holds a fiddle and a bow on his knee as he looks lovingly at his companion who sits with an open Bible in her lap and knitting needles in her gnarled hands. The two figures are bent and worn, but appear unmistakably happy. The years they wear seem to slip away, and love shines from their faces.

The couple depicted in the statue are Peter and Celestia Petersen. Both were raised and buried in Fairview, Utah. Peter was the first boy born in Fairview—then known as North Bend—and Celestia was born three months later, the third child born in the town. The childhood sweethearts were married in December 1878 in St. George, Utah. It took them eight days by wagon to make the 300-mile journey from Fairview to St. George. The couple "cousined" their way home, staying with relatives along the way.

The first of ten children was born to Peter and Celestia in December 1879. At their eightieth wedding anniversary in 1958, their posterity numbered 252, including twenty-eight great-great-grandchildren. *Life Magazine* featured the couple in its January 5, 1959, issue, illustrating the article with photographs of the 200 family members who were able to attend the anniversary party. Two years later, at the age of 100 years, Peter died. Celestia followed him a year later, just a month shy of her 101st birthday.

Celestia's mother, Sarah Vail Terry, taught her daughter to sew and quilt as a little girl. When Celestia was twelve, the two of them made this Feathered Star quilt together. The turkey red cotton fabric of the star is quilted in red thread, and the green cotton blocks that surround the star are quilted in green, seven stitches to the inch, in flowers, wreaths, and crosshatching; the centers of the green squares are quilted with a large circle and smaller comma shapes facing clockwise and counterclockwise. The double border is striking, consisting of a small red and green sawtooth inner border and a two-inch red outer border. The applied binding is green. The quilt back was pieced from flour sacks dyed light blue. Celestia and Sarah hand carded the wool batting that is inside the quilt.

This quilt must have been a "best quilt," for it shows little wear. Leah Larsen has now donated her grandmother's cherished quilt to the museum in Fairview. It hangs alongside the statue that honors her grandparents.

1872

Feathered Star

88" x 68"

Cotton Muslin

Made by Celestia Melissa Terry Petersen

(1860–1961) and

Sarah Vail Terry (1818–1917)

Made in Fairview, Sanpete County, Utah

Owned by Leah Larsen

Eliza
Rowberry
Nelson

■ ■

The story of this quilt is the story of two sisters, Mary Ann and Harriet Gollaher, six years apart in age but always close in heart and habit. Both women were quilters and both women were married to John Rowberry, a British convert to the L.D.S. church and an early settler of Tooele, Utah. Though much is known about Bishop John Rowberry, it is difficult to tease out the story of his wives from the pages of history. Only the barest of facts are known, but much can be deduced from the delicate Flower Vase quilt the sisters pieced and quilted together for their stepdaughter Eliza. There is a sense of harmony and of balance evident in this quilt, perhaps a reflection of the women who created it.

Mary Ann Gollaher was born in Illinois in 1829 to Elizabeth Orton and William Gollaher. The Gollaher family was originally from Georgia, moving to Illinois when they joined the L.D.S. church and later migrating to Utah. Mary Ann probably met John Rowberry in Tooele, where he had lived since 1849, working for Ezra Taft Benson as a livestock supervisor.

When Mary Ann married him in 1853, John was newly widowed with six children to care for, ranging in age from fourteen to the infant Eliza, just six months old when her mother died of a lung ailment. Mary Ann eventually bore John ten more children. After three years of marriage to Mary Ann, John Rowberry took his third wife, Mary Ann's younger sister Harriet Frances Gollaher. Harriet raised her ten children in Grantsville, a town a short distance from Tooele.

When Eliza announced her forthcoming marriage to William Nelson, her elated stepmothers celebrated by choosing a pattern for her wedding quilt top. Eliza's quilt is a Flower Vase Applique done in red and green on white. The vibrant tulips fairly dance across the quilt top, bursting from vases hardly large enough to hold them. It is a joyous design, full of life and love and good wishes. Eliza cherished the quilt until her death in 1949, when it was bequeathed to her daughter Bertha Tripp. Eliza's grandson and his wife now own the quilt.

After Eliza's marriage, Ann and Harriet continued their quiet, busy lives of quilting and gardening and raising children; John became mayor of Tooele. In 1876 he served a short L.D.S. mission to England. In 1884 he died at the age of sixty. Mary passed away six years later, and Harriet lived until 1929, outliving four of her children. It is not known whether any other quilts designed by the Gollaher sisters survive.

Before 1873

Flower Vase Applique

68" x 88"

Cotton

Made by Mary Ann Gollaher Rowberry
(1829–1900) and Harriet Gollaher
Rowberry (1823–1929)
Made in Tooele, Tooele County, Utah
Owned by Helen W. Tripp

Eliza
Luff
Crossland
Banks

Carmen Martinez did not think any of her great-grandmother's quilts had survived through the years. Eliza Banks had been a very thrifty woman, trained by a life of hardship and poverty to use, remake, reuse, and discard a thing only when it fell apart. Knowing her grandmother's habits, Carmen was certain that any quilts she had made would have been used to extinction long ago. But during a visit with a quilt group to the Daughters of Utah Pioneers Museum in Pleasant Grove, Utah, to see the antique quilt collection, Carmen discovered the one surviving testament to her great-grandmother's skill with a needle. She wept when she realized it was Eliza's quilt.

Eliza Luff Crossland was born on Red Lion Street in London, England, on June 6, 1851. When she was two years old, the family sold all its belongings and sailed to America. While crossing the plains, Eliza's father died and was hastily buried near Green River, Wyoming. Her mother, Frances, continued the journey westward with her four daughters, the youngest one only a few months old.

Frances Crossland managed to earn a scanty living in Salt Lake by working in shops and homes, probably cooking or sewing, to provide the barest of necessities for her little girls. In 1859, she married William Adams of Pleasant Grove. He had three children from a previous marriage as well as a blind and almost helpless mother. Together he and Frances had three more children, eventually becoming a family of thirteen in a single room. Two of the boys slept in the granary under a single buffalo robe, somewhat easing the congestion, but one wonders how they survived the winters. Not everyone in the family had shoes; no one had enough clothing or food. Even at the best of times their diet consisted mainly of bread, bacon, and potatoes.

Eliza began "working out" in other people's homes when she was eight years old. She earned her living this way until her marriage to Franklin Cyrus Banks in 1869. Schooling for the young pioneer girl was an elusive dream, consisting of three or four three-month terms of formal education. Eliza's son Junius describes her school equipment as consisting of one Wilson Reader, one elementary speller, and a slate. Not until after she married Franklin did Eliza learn to write, and then only after great effort.

When Eliza was thirty-four years old, her husband was called by L.D.S. church leaders to serve a two-year mission, leaving his pregnant wife with seven young children, a farm to manage, and horses and cattle to look after. The farm was let out on shares to other farmers; Eliza was to receive 50 percent of the yield. As it turned out, the food produced on the farm decreased by 50 percent because the ground had been poorly tilled, and the family had only one-fourth of what they were used to. Nevertheless, Eliza fed and clothed her children and somehow managed to send money to her husband in the mission field. It was not without a price. Her eighth child was stillborn, perhaps because of the added chores and worries she faced.

In 1886, Eliza suffered a terrible accident that took its toll on her health for many years. She and three of her children were on their way to Salt Lake City in a buggy drawn by an unmanageable horse aptly named "Danger." When the reins were transferred from Eliza to her son Frank, the horse felt the restraint slacken and bolted forward at an uncontrollable speed. Eliza seized the reins again and turned the horse toward some railroad tracks. The children were thrown from the buggy, for the most part uninjured, but Eliza, still holding the reins, was dragged over the rails. For two days, she lay unconscious, surrounded by relatives who had come to say their final good-byes. She miraculously awoke at the close of the third day to begin a slow and painful recovery. Three years passed before her mental capabilities were restored.

Franklin returned from his mission in the fall of 1887. Although Eliza's mind continued to improve, her physical condition deteriorated, causing her to spend her days in bed. Many doctors were consulted and it was decided that an operation was Eliza's only chance at life, even though at that time such a cure was often much worse than the illness. Eliza survived the surgery and made a full recovery. One of her friends told her, "Oh, you'll live forever and then turn into a buckskin string."

Eliza was widowed at the age of seventy-one when Franklin suffered his third stroke. She lived alone until her failing health and memory made it necessary for her to live with her grown children. As the years passed by, she began to imagine herself in the days of her childhood, living now with strange people she didn't recognize, begging to be taken to her own people. She passed away at the age of eighty-eight.

Carmen will use her own remarkable quilt-making skills in fulfilling her dream of reproducing the beautiful Feathered Star quilt her great-grandmother made so many years ago.

1875

Feathered Star

78″ x 78″

Cotton

Made by Eliza Luff Crossland Banks

(1851–1940)

Made in Lindon, Utah County, Utah

Owned by the Daughters of Utah

Pioneers Museum, Pleasant Grove, Utah

■ ■

Elvira
Pamela
Mills
Cox

Sheep still graze in the fields of Fairview, Utah, just as they did in the early 1880s when Elvira Pamela Mills Cox stitched this serviceable quilt. To the hard-working Cox family, sheep were a storehouse, providing tallow for candles and soap, mutton for meals, and wool for the spinning and weaving at which Elvira excelled.

Elvira Pamela (pronounced Pam-ē´-la) Mills was born in Nelson, Ohio, March 2, 1820, the oldest of two children born to Robert Mills and Rhoda Hulet. When Robert died in 1827, Rhoda looked to her younger brother Sylvester Hulet for help. A remarkable man, Uncle Sylvester assumed the care and support of Rhoda and her children, his widowed sister Charlotte and her three children, and the only child of his brother Francis, whose wife had died in childbirth. Sylvester was a professional weaver and spinner and could usually obtain food for the family on short notice by hiring out as a weaver.

In 1831, Elvira and many of her Hulet relatives were baptized into the newly organized L.D.S. church. Two years later, Elvira's family and neighbors were driven from their homes in Jackson County, Missouri, by vigilante mobs. The next fourteen years would be spent searching through Ohio, Missouri, and Illinois for a permanent home, leading at last to the safety and isolation of the Salt Lake Valley.

During the terrible move from Far West, Missouri, to Illinois in the winter of 1838–39, Elvira met Orville Cox, a young blacksmith and engineer who could "make dams hold in quicksand." His singing and laughter lifted her spirits through the cold and muddy days. Elvira loved him from the start, but refused to marry him because he was not a Mormon. Orville was baptized into the L.D.S. church three days after their wedding on October 3, 1839. Two sons and a daughter were born to the couple in Illinois, the first child living only one week.

In 1847, the Cox family headed west with the Mormon pioneers. While traveling along the Sweetwater River in Wyoming, they met Elvira's beloved uncle, now Lieutenant Sylvester Hulet, who was returning from California after a year of service with the Mormon Battalion. He was discharged on the spot and allowed to join Elvira and her family on their trek. They arrived in the valley of the Great Salt Lake in September 1847. In November, Elvira gave birth to her third son, Orville. According to family history, he was the sixth child born in the fort at Salt Lake and the first male child born in the Salt Lake Valley to Utah pioneers to live to maturity.

Elvira was a plural wife, as were so many of her Mormon contemporaries. Her husband had taken a second wife in 1853 and a third in 1859. Elvira was in charge of making clothing for Orville's ever-expanding family, a task she was well suited for. The Hulet family of New England had long been "spinsters," spinning and weaving flax into linen for personal use and barter. Elvira was no exception, though now it was wool she carded for batting and spun into fine thread for her sturdy twills and soft homespun.

By 1854 Orville had built Elvira a loom for her home in Manti, Utah, where the family had settled in 1849. Most likely she had brought the precious metal "loom irons" with her across the plains. She taught her children to spin on a five-foot-high "walking wheel" with a counter to keep track of the yardage. (A walking wheel is a spinning wheel without a treadle; the wheel is turned by hand. Each time the spinner turns the wheel she then walks away from it as she drafts a fine thread from the carded wool in her left hand.) Grandson Orville Cox Day recorded the following about Grandma Elvira, who would give her grandchildren a piece of squash pie or a cookie when they visited, then put them to work: "At age four, we could wind yarn into a ball or stamp wool to clean it in a homemade tub with homemade soap, and afterward pick the dry chunks of wool to pieces. At seven we could card it into bats for quilts; at ten, card the bats into rolls for spinning; at eleven, knit socks; at twelve, spin; and at thirteen we could weave."

In 1865, Orville, an expert on irrigation, was called by L.D.S. church leaders to open a new Mormon mission on the Muddy River in Nevada. Elvira did not join him there until 1868. Her reluctance to move to an uncertain future in Nevada stemmed in part from her practicality. In a letter to Orville dated July 29, 1867, she wrote, "It don't seem to me that peaches, molasses and the agu will compensate for good health, good water, potatoes, bread, milk, butter, beef and etc., but I will let you be the judge in these matters."

She returned home to Utah when the mission was closed in 1872, ill from bad water and the heat and exhausted from the hardship. Five of the Cox children and one grandchild had died while the family lived on the Muddy. She later wrote that she would "rather drown a hundred times than die of thirst" in the deserts of Nevada. Elvira spent the final thirty-one years of her life in Fairview, a small town north of

Manti, near her nine remaining children. In 1903 she was buried beside Orville and her Uncle Sylvester in the Fairview Cemetery.

Elvira's time-worn quilt tells more about her than any photograph or journal entry could. This quilt reflects her standards of thrift and resourcefulness: Every inch of fabric on the quilt top was woven by the quiltmaker. There are twill squares saved from the least worn sections of Orville's threadbare pants, homespun from a wool petticoat or cape, plaids and checks and stripes patched over and sewn onto other patches. Apparently, nothing of any possible use was overlooked. It is not surprising to learn that at the age of seventy-two Elvira was still saving every scrap of bread for fear of famine, toasting it and hanging it in flour sacks in the attic.

This quilt is also a tribute, a memorial to Elvira's Uncle Sylvester, the man who became her father, who taught her to weave, who returned again and again to his family in the West, settling in Manti to be near them, and dying in the home of his beloved niece in 1885. Sylvester wove the sturdy red and blue plaid cloth that backs the quilt. It was the traveling blanket he used as a bedroll and poncho as he guided wagon trains of Mormons moving west. When it became too worn to keep him warm and dry and he became too old and ill to need it, Elvira cut and stitched the blanket and made it a part of her quilt, just as Uncle Sylvester had always been a part of her life.

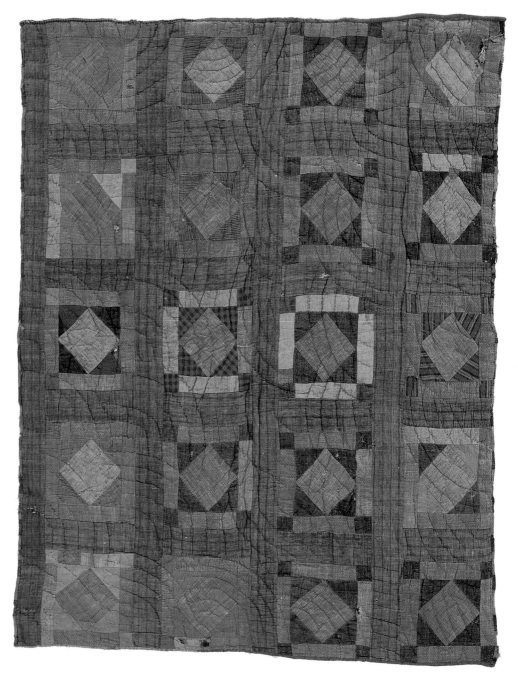

Early 1880s

New Album

67" x 84"

Wool

Made by Elvira Pamela Mills Cox

(1820–1903)

Made in Fairview, Sanpete County, Utah

Owned by Lee T. Cox

Mary Alice Klingensmith was eleven years old when her father left his family. Her mother, Betsy Cattle, died a short time later in 1869, leaving four daughters between the ages of eight and thirteen in the care of an aunt. Three months into the new living arrangement, the aunt passed away. The two youngest girls went to live with relatives; Mary Alice and her older sister Priscilla were left alone.

The sisters somehow managed to stay together in their home, learning by experience all the tasks necessary to keep life going. There were friends and relatives nearby to lend moral support, but nothing in the way of financial assistance was possible. The two girls went to work for anyone who would hire them to wash clothes, scrub floors, even pick mulberry leaves, which they did for a neighbor involved in the fledgling silk industry in southern Utah. They sometimes received a yard of calico fabric for a day's work.

Mary Alice probably learned to stitch that calico into a dress through trial and error, the same as she was learning everything else. At the age of twelve, she made her first dress, taking the pattern from an old dress she had carefully picked apart and calculating the adjustments she needed to make so the new dress would fit her for another year or two. This first attempt at sewing undoubtedly opened the door to Mary Alice's lifelong fascination with fabrics and design. She was soon hired by John Middleton to sew for his large family. He paid her by giving her credit on a sewing machine that she used to support herself with her exceptional skills at sewing both men's and women's clothing.

When she wasn't sewing, Mary Alice and her sister had a second business making straw hats. They gathered straw from fields or rushes and reeds from riverbanks to weave and braid into hats. For three successive years they took first place in the county fair with their hats. They also provided the women of Cedar City with a very fashionable way to shade themselves from the sun.

At the age of fourteen, Mary Alice was called on to make burial clothes for the deceased in the community. She devoted herself to this service for over sixty years, helping to lay over one thousand individuals to rest.

Mary Alice married John Benson, a handsome Latter-day Saint convert from England, when she was twenty-three. They traveled for three days to marry in the St. George L.D.S. Temple on November 24, 1880, camping in the sagebrush and cooking their meals over an open fire. They settled in Parowan, a small town twenty miles northeast of her native Cedar City, raising ten children, eight of whom lived to adulthood. John was a farmer, and Mary Alice continued to sew, adding quilting, crocheting, weaving, and clothing alterations to her seemingly endless list of talents. When she was past seventy-eight years of age, she made a quilt for each of her children.

The Princess Feather quilt was made by Mary Alice sometime before her wedding in 1880. It is a remarkable example of a nearly perfect applique technique. The colored pieces of the design appear to be woven into the fabric rather than stitched onto it. The magnificent colors were hand dyed, and still retain a vibrance that belies the quilt's age. One interesting feature of the quilt is the border with blue stems and leaves. Her granddaughter LaBerta Whitlock thinks Mary Alice may have run out of green dye or had extra blue fabric or blue dye she wanted to use.

Whatever the reason, the unusual plants add a surreal charm to the quilt.

Mary Alice died in 1937, one month after her eightieth birthday.

Mary
Alice
Klingensmith
Benson

Before 1880

Princess Feather

76" x 77"

Cotton

Made by Mary Alice Klingensmith Benson
(1857–1937)

Made in Cedar City, Iron County, Utah

Owned by LaBerta Whitlock

Ruth
Ridge
Moses

■ ■

Ruth Ridge was a little girl of eleven when her father was struck by lightning and killed during their journey to join the Mormons in Utah. It was about 1850, and Ruth, who had already helped to bury her mother in the family's native England, was frightened and alone on the plains. She managed to reach Salt Lake with the help of friends, but where she lived or how is not known.

When she was a young woman, she found employment at the home of a middle-aged couple named Julian and Barbara Matilda Moses. Barbara was crippled and unable to have children and, being older than Ruth, must have seemed a motherly figure to her. Ruth worked for them for a short time before becoming Julian's second wife on February 12, 1857. She was eighteen years old; Julian was almost forty-seven.

In December 1857, Ruth gave birth to her first child, a son whom she named Julian Neff; Neff was Barbara's maiden name. According to family history, Ruth gave the baby boy to Barbara to raise as her own son, which she did until the young man's death in 1875. Ruth also had three daughters, the last born in 1875 when Julian was sixty-five years old.

Ruth was well known as a midwife, for which services she charged two dollars, if the family could pay. She would usually stay with the mother for several days to help out with the new baby.

In 1881, Ruth's oldest daughter, named Barbara Matilda after the first wife, was married to Horace Cummings. Ruth gave her this beautiful Carpenter's Wheel quilt, which the two had worked on together. It is a precise design, especially dramatic in the simple color scheme chosen by them. The pattern is also known as Double Star, Star-within-a-Star, and Dutch Rose.

The gridlike effect of the green sashing is echoed in the quilted grid design of the red and green border. The outline of the pieced shapes is quilted in tiny, even stitches. Although some of the sashing has faded, which is natural for green fabric of that age, the quilt is still in superior condition.

Ruth lost her dear friend and mentor, Barbara, in 1890, and her husband two years later. She lived into her seventieth year, dying in Salt Lake City on January 29, 1910.

1881

Carpenter's Wheel

84″ x 85″

Cotton

Made by Ruth Ridge Moses (1839–1910)

Made in Salt Lake City, Salt Lake County,

Utah

Owned by LaJean Cummings

Julia Ann Collett Cantwell

Like most children dressed up in their Sunday best, Patricia Michaud was always anxious to change out of her dress after church. In her family, they called it getting "out of the agony," a term dating back to pioneer times and her great-grandmother Julia Ann Cantwell. It was "out of the agony" every Sunday, "out of the agony" after a wedding or a funeral, "out of the agony" as fast as possible. Like Patricia, Julia may not have enjoyed dressing up, but she knew what to do with a fancy dress or a handsome tie that had seen better days. Into the scrapbag it went, to be carefully taken apart and snipped into rectangular strips to use in constructing an elegant Log Cabin quilt that would cause agony for no one.

Julia Ann is thought to have pieced and quilted this opulent bed covering in 1881, the year before she gave birth to the fifth of her nine children. She used scraps from velvet dress bodices she and her little daughter had worn out, salvaged pieces from her husband's suits, even tucked away satin hair ribbons with an inch or two of use left in them. The quilt was probably brought out only for special occasions as evidenced by the rich, royal colors and excellent condition of the fabrics.

Julia Ann Collett was the ninth child born to Daniel and Esther Jones Collett. The couple were married in 1833 in England and joined the L.D.S. church several years later. On May 10, 1841, the family sailed on the *Harmony* from Bristol, England, to Quebec, Canada. They settled in Nauvoo, Illinois, until the expulsion of the Mormons to Iowa in 1846. For several years Daniel remained in Winter Quarters, the Mormon way station on the Missouri River, working as a wheelwright until 1849, when he was able to move his family to the Salt Lake Valley. In 1851, Julia was born in Mill Creek, the first Collett child born in Utah. When Julia was six years old, her mother died after giving birth to her eleventh child. Daniel remarried shortly thereafter, eventually taking six additional wives in plural marriage.

Julia spent most of her childhood in Lehi, Utah, where her parents had moved after her birth. Daniel was a prominent citizen in the little pioneer town, serving on the city council, on the first school board, and as water master. In the spring of 1860, the time was right for more pioneering for the Collett family. They were among the group of original settlers of Summit, later renamed Smithfield, eight miles north of Logan, Utah. After a raid by Shoshone Indians in July 1860 that left two settlers dead, most of the early homes were subsequently built close together in fortlike lines. For many months, the men worked in groups to increase their safety whenever they left the fort.

In 1872, at the age of twenty-one, Julia married a handsome Englishman named James Cantwell, eight years her senior. She had known James and his father from when they first settled in Smithfield in 1862. James had been born in Liverpool, England, in 1843, and was seven years old when the family left England for America. Six years later, the Cantwells joined the Willie Handcart Company, crossing the plains to Utah in 1856. Both James and his father were given two town lots and a small piece of acreage to farm when they settled in Smithfield. Ten years later, Julia moved with James to his farm, where they raised their nine children. Together they worked the farm and ran a mercantile store in Smithfield until James's death in 1922.

There is little doubt Julia made many more quilts than Patricia's Log Cabin, for it is well known that she loved to attend quilting bees. There was always socializing and renewing of old friendships and food—lots of food—since any proper quilting bee also had a good-natured cooking competition to see who excelled in the kitchen. The quilt was given to Julia's daughter Lenora Kirkbride, who had no children and later gave the quilt to her niece Elthura Merrill, the mother of the present quilt owner, Patricia Michaud. Patricia remembers seeing the quilt once or twice every year during her childhood when Great-Aunt Lenora pulled it from the trunk just to give her a peek. Patricia was thrilled to know that it would belong to her someday. In 1979, she became the owner.

1881

Log Cabin

70″ x 77½″

Cotton, silk, and wool

Made by Julia Ann Collett Cantwell

(1851–1934)

Made in Smithfield, Cache County, Utah

Owned by Patricia Michaud

Anna
Lowrie
Ivins

Nine-year-old Anthony Ivins raced home to announce the dreadful news to his mother and sister. "Mama, the Moodys are called to Dixie. President Young wants them to go. They have to leave Salt Lake and grow cotton and . . ." His voice trailed off as he noticed the tears in his mother's eyes. "So are we!" his sister sobbed. "So are we!"

The Cotton Mission of 1861 consisted of 309 families sent to the southern part of the Utah territory—called "Utah's Dixie" because of its warm and mild climate—to establish permanent communities and grow cotton. Many of the settlers were originally from the southern states and were skilled in such horticultural endeavors. The Ivins family had its origins in Pennsylvania and New Jersey, but Israel Ivins was a surveyor and a doctor, both essential to a new settlement.

Israel and Anna Ivins were second cousins, great-grandchildren of Moses and Kezia Ivins. For generations, the family had been devout members of the Religious Society of Friends. They called themselves Friends, but their enemies called them Quakers to mock the fact that they urged unbelievers to tremble at the word of God.

Wealthy merchants, landowners, and scholars fill the Ivins family rosters on both sides. Although Anna's parents died when she was young, she was raised in comfort and luxury by a well-to-do cousin. At the age of twenty-three she joined the L.D.S. church and was disowned by her wealthy brothers. She married Israel in 1844 and the two settled in Tom's River, New Jersey. Two daughters and a

son were born to them—Caroline, Georgiana (who died at four months of age), and Anthony.

In 1853, the family set out by mule train for the Salt Lake Valley, making the happily uneventful trip in 128 days. They had established a comfortable life after eight years in Salt Lake City when the call to move to Utah's Dixie came from church leaders. In the fall of 1861, Israel sold the house and property, bought two yoke of oxen, a heavy prairie schooner, and a light one-horse wagon, and with Anna and the two children began the month-long journey south. They descended into the valley on the first of December, with only two families arriving ahead of them. On January 15, 1862, Israel began surveying the site for the city of St. George, where he and his family would reside for the rest of their lives.

The settlers in Utah's Dixie lived in tents and wagon boxes for the first year, enduring high winds and heavy rains. In 1862, the Ivins family moved to the new townsite, settling on a homestead lot that would eventually be occupied by a tall, ivy-covered house surrounded by fruit and almond trees, grape arbors, and flower gardens.

Family, church, and needlework were the mainstays of Anna Lowrie Ivins's life. Her granddaughter and namesake, Anna Lowrie Wilson, wrote of the beautiful embroidery, netting, and needlework her grandmother produced: "My mother's babies possessed many articles of clothing, made and adorned by [my grandmother's] hand, little net dresses and aprons to wear over bright colored dresses, beautifully embroidered flannel petticoats and shoulder blankets. Our house was decorated with net pillow shams, fancy splashers and framed samplers all the work of her hands."

Anna Lowrie Wilson was especially proud of the Crazy Patch quilt her grandmother completed for her in 1886. The quilt was probably designed to fit a settee, and is constructed of thirteen squares, each approximately eleven inches to a side, with smaller squares filling in the eight corners. Images are painted and embroidered onto the silk and velvet crazy-patch pieces that make up the squares. There are butterflies, a mockingbird, raspberries, pansies, a horse, and a cat. Kate Greenaway-like motifs of a small boy, a girl, and a goose join company with birds, an umbrella, a horseshoe, an anchor, and the letter L. One square showcases the tools of Anna's art—a pair of spectacles, scissors, thimble, and needle and thread. The center square is embroidered with the statement, "Made by A. L. Ivins in her 70th year 1886." Anna Ivins particularly treasured a piece of fabric in the quilt, said to be a scrap from one of Queen Victoria's gowns, that a friend had brought her from England. In a life filled with hardship, sacrifice, and disappointment, including the death of her daughter Caroline two years earlier, this quilt shines with the joy of a woman who celebrated the simple blessings of each day.

In 1895, Anthony Ivins was called to Old Mexico to preside over the Mormon colonies in northern Chihua-hua. Both Anna and Israel dreaded this separation from their only living child, knowing that at their advanced ages it would be impossible for them to make such a long trip. On January 11, 1896, while Anthony was in Mexico preparing for his move, Anna Lowrie Ivins passed away after a short illness. Her son paid tribute to her in this way: "The one thing which impressed me most in the character of my mother was, that during . . . poverty and different family

1886

Crazy Patch

56″ x 58½″

Silk and velvet

Made by Anna Lowrie Ivins (1816–1896)

Made in St. George, Washington County, Utah

Custodian, Anna Lowrie Anderson

England

conditions from those to which she had been accustomed in her early life, she did not for a moment lose her patience, dignity or self control. She was the same dignified, patient, pleasant woman under all circumstances."

Harriet
Elizabeth
Ford
Thorley

Seventeen-year old Hattie Ford took great care in choosing the colors and fabrics for the quilt that would be the central feature of her trousseau—mint green, turkey red, and two prints, one with tiny black stars on a white background, the other resembling little black paw prints on a snow-white field. With the help of her mother, Martha Jane Mulliner Ford, she cut and pieced and stitched the hours away. In the center of the quilt, she embroidered her initials and the year 1889, then readied the wooden quilting frame. She secured pale blue muslin to the frame and layered it with cotton batting, then spread the flawlessly executed feathered stars on top and began quilting. Ten perfect stitches to the inch she took, using white thread on the white fabric, green on green, and red on red. In the plain green squares she quilted a feathered wreath; all other pieces she outlined with her tiny stitches, adding crosshatching to the circle within each star. She stitched red binding around the edges of the quilt, being especially careful to keep the corners square, then tucked it away for the day of her marriage.

On May 10, 1891, she married William A. Thorley from Cedar City, Utah, and lovingly unpacked the quilt she had made for this day. Its warm colors and intricate stitching seemed the perfect symbol for the way their hearts and lives had joined together.

Hattie's life was not to be as precise and organized as her beautiful quilt. Not long after their wedding, Will took sick and died of the flu, leaving her a widow at the age of nineteen. She soon discovered she was carrying Will's child. The long winter hours were passed stitching clothing for the new baby, expected sometime in the spring.

Shortly before the birth of her baby, Hattie learned that her own mother would be having a baby at the end of the year—a new brother or sister to be raised with her own child. How exciting it would be to share this experience with her mother and to hand down the baby clothes after her baby outgrew them. Hattie delivered her baby on schedule in the spring of 1892, but the baby died at birth; and on June 10, 1892, just one year and one month from the day of her marriage, Hattie died too. (No one has been able to identify the cause of her death.)

Martha Jane Ford gave birth to her ninth baby on December 23, 1892. She used Hattie's untouched baby clothes to dress her new daughter, Genevieve, Hattie's little sister. She wrapped up the red and green feathered star quilt and put it away for Genevieve to have when she was older. When Genevieve died in 1981, the quilt was given to her daughter, DeVona, who recalls that the quilt was always special to her family and only brought out for special occasions. "Hattie's Quilt" is all that is left of a little pioneer family from 1892.

1889

Feathered Star

76" x 63"

Cotton

Made by Harriet Elizabeth Ford Thorley

(1872–1892)

Made in Kanarraville, Iron County, Utah

Owned by DeVona K. Griffiths

Mary
Ann
Ford
Simmons

Mary Ann Ford was born into a privileged English family on November 25, 1827. Her schooling was provided through a private tutor until the death of her mother when Mary Ann was fourteen years old. She moved to Brighton, where she lived with her brother for two years until starting a school for small children in 1843 at the age of sixteen. Six years later, on Christmas Eve, she married a carpenter named George Simmons.

It was George who first introduced Mary Ann to the L.D.S. church. One of his employees, a Mormon named Henry Hollist, would stand on a keg and preach during the lunch hour. George took Mary Ann to hear him, and she would later say that as she listened to him she knew it was what she had been looking for. The family was baptized and soon prepared to leave England for the Mormon Zion in the Mountain West. In 1855, Mary Ann, George, little George William, and two-year-old Mary Ann set sail on an old ship named the *Chrimborazo*. Since they were steerage passengers, the going was rough on "the old tub" as Mary Ann called it. She writes that it was miserable from the first day to the last, sometimes too much wind and other times not enough. How thankful they were to land in Philadelphia.

The family traveled over the Allegheny Mountains in the cattle car of a train, then sailed on the Mississippi and Missouri rivers, which Mary Ann described as being joined together as you would put two flat pieces of wood or fabric beside one another. One river was clear as could be, the other as thick as mud. They spent a night in St. Louis

where they met a man they had known in England who took them home with him for the day and fed them three wonderful meals. The next day they went to Mormon Grove, to prepare for the trip across the plains.

George and Mary became part of the Richard Ballentine oxteam company of emigrants. As they traveled west, they watched millions of grasshoppers moving eastward. For days they passed the swarming insects, sometimes so thick in the sky they hid the sun. On August 16, just outside of Laramie, Wyoming, Mary Ann gave birth to a son who lived only half an hour and was buried on the plains. The family arrived in the Salt Lake Valley on September 25, 1855.

Life in Zion was one trial after another for the pioneers. There was nothing to eat, the grasshoppers having eaten anything that hadn't died in the drought. There was no firewood. Mary Ann kept her family alive for two months on frozen potatoes and the coarsest siftings of cornmeal. A neighbor, Sophronia Martin, often made hot milk thickened with flour and invited the Simmons family over for dinner. Every evening she would bring a cup of milk, still warm from the cow, to Mary Ann's daughter, who eventually recovered from an illness that lasted through that first winter in Utah. When spring came, Mary gathered sego lily bulbs and planted a garden. She took in sewing to trade for food for her family.

In 1861, George and Mary Ann moved their family to Morgan, Utah. Their log house had a dirt floor and a dirt roof; she often commented that when it quit raining outside, it would continue to rain in the house. For seven years they were plagued with grasshoppers whose eggs, laid one year, would hatch the next, with apparently

no way to stop them. George continued his carpentry business, as well as farming, and was called on to make all the coffins for that part of the territory. Mary Ann took on the pioneer home-making jobs—carding and spinning wool, weaving fabric, and making starch from potatoes, molasses from beets, and currant preserves with molasses because there was no sugar. The family eventually moved into the first brick house in Morgan County, a "palace" with seven rooms and a garden overflowing with apples, plums, gooseberries, currants, rhubarb, and strawberries.

Mary Ann stitched the Log Cabin quilt in 1890 for the wedding of her daughter Julia to James William Walker. The blocks are set on point, an unusual setting for a sunshine and shadows pattern. The quilt was taken to Antelope Island in the Great Salt Lake, where the couple lived for thirteen years. Will raised the first buffalo herd on the island.

In 1898, following the death of her husband, Mary Ann traveled to Australia to visit her brother. She was gone for a year and returned again several years later. Although she was not officially called to do so, she became the first Latter-day Saint missionary in Williamstown, Australia. Mary Ann left Australia in 1907 and died in Morgan at the age of ninety-two.

1890

**Log Cabin, Sunshine and
Shadow Setting**

78½" x 89¼"

Cotton

Made by Mary Ann Ford Simmons

(1827–1920)

Made in Morgan, Morgan County, Utah

Owned by Noreen Olsen

In 1842, a small group of women met in the home of Sarah M. Kimball to organize a sewing society they thought might benefit the men working on construction of the Nauvoo L.D.S. temple. When they asked the Prophet Joseph Smith to endorse their under-taking, he suggested an alternative that would "furnish the sisters of the Church an organization through which they may actively foster the welfare of the members." It would be designed to "aid the poor, nurse the sick and afflicted, and . . . engage in true charitable work in behalf of all whose necessities require assistance." On March 17, 1842, he established the Female Relief Society of Nauvoo, known ever since as the Relief Society. Twenty women were present, including Martha McBride Knight, who spent her thirty-seventh birthday in that historical first meeting of the oldest auxiliary organization in the Latter-day Saint church.

Martha Knight was born in 1805 in Chester, New York, to Daniel and Abigail Mead McBride. She married Vinson Knight of Maine in 1826 and together they had seven children. Vinson was a bishop in Nauvoo, Illinois, and prominent in the business affairs of the church, being called upon many times to transact land purchases in the area. Only four months after Martha's attendance at the first Relief Society meeting, Vinson fell ill and died at the age of thirty-eight, leaving Martha to raise six children; one son had died five years earlier. Less than two months after Vinson's death, her youngest child, eleven-month-old Rodolphus, died. In 1844, she buried her five-year-old daughter, Martha Abigail.

Martha and her children remained in Nauvoo until the Mormons were driven from their homes in early 1846, settling temporarily on the banks of the Missouri River at Winter Quarters. Death was everywhere and provisions were scarce. The people survived chiefly on corn and pork, and the lack of fresh vegetables caused much illness and fatigue. Seven hundred log cabins and 150 dugouts were built during the two-year period the Mormons inhabited Winter Quarters, Nebraska. In 1848, the settlement was abandoned by the church, and many of those members who were not yet able to leave for the Salt Lake Valley moved to the east side of the Missouri River, settling in a town they called Kanesville (later, Council Bluffs).

Martha and her teenage son, James, left Iowa in 1850 along with her daughter and son-in-law, Adaline and Gilbert Belnap. The family originally settled in Ogden, Utah, but over the next fifty-one years, Martha lived in Hooper, Springville, Fillmore, Santa Clara, and the Cache Valley. She stayed with her children or other relatives and friends.

The quilt top Martha made in 1891 for her granddaughter Adaline is a treasured family heirloom. Adaline never had it quilted because she prized the fine stitching; every fourth stitch in the hand-pieced top is backstitched. However, when Adaline's daughter Zeruah inherited the quilt top, she decided to quilt it, and many of Adaline's descendants put in a few stitches. The pattern was known on the frontier as Bear Paw or Duck's Foot in the Mud. In Pennsylvania the Quakers called it Hand of Friendship. The family name for the pattern is "Double Houndstooth." Martha stitched her design using three different red prints: a small red and white stripe, a tiny red on red floral print, and a pale red stripe overlaid with intertwined circles. The blocks are set together with light yellow sashing and deep green connecting blocks, both of which are used in the border.

Martha Knight's stitching mastery began when she learned to sew as a child. At the age of thirteen, she won a prize at the New York State Fair for sewing the best buttonholes. Sewing and quilting remained a constant in Martha's long life. The Bear Paw quilt was sewn when Martha was eighty-six years old and living in Hooper. She died ten years later, leaving her large family a tangible heritage of faith and beauty.

Martha

McBride

Knight

1891

Bear Paw

71" x 84"

Cotton

Made by Martha McBride Knight

(1805–1901)

Made in Hooper, Weber County, Utah

Owned by the Zeruah Lowe Thomson

family

When Sarah Ann Howard joined the L.D.S. church and married Isaac Laney in 1841, her family disowned her. So, with only a spinning wheel and a horse, she left Blue Grass, Kentucky, and settled in Illinois with Isaac. In 1847 the family, now including a son and a daughter, joined the Hunter Company of pioneers and traveled to the Salt Lake Valley, where they lived for the remainder of their lives.

Sarah Ann Howard was born into Southern wealth and comfort. The horse she took with her across the plains, that pulled her wagon in the stifling heat, was a Kentucky thoroughbred. It broke her heart to work him so hard, but Sarah Ann always did the needful thing, and the beautiful horse seemed to understand and forgive.

Sarah Ann gave birth to another daughter and three sons in Salt Lake. They loved to listen to their parents tell stories about their trek across the plains or their troubles with the mobs in Illinois. Isaac must have told his children about the day he survived the Haun's Mill Massacre on October 30, 1838. He was a wheelwright by trade and was in the mill when the mob began to fire. The stock of his gun was shot to pieces as he held it in his hands. He ran from the mill with bullets whistling around him. He was shot eleven times, but there were twenty-seven bullet holes in his shirt, seven in his pants, and his coat was cut to shreds. He ran into a nearby house, where he was hidden under the floor until the mob had left. The blood gushing from his mouth nearly strangled him.

Of Sarah Ann's and Isaac's six children, all but one lived to adulthood. Little Isaac Jefferson died in 1852 at the age of seventeen months; a year later, Joseph Laney was born, and six years after that Hyrum, the youngest child, was born. It was Hyrum who inherited Sarah Ann's Chimney Sweep quilt after her death in 1902. In 1929, Great-uncle Hyrum brought the quilt to his niece Ruth, transferring ownership to her. As a lawyer with no children of his own, he had, "after due consideration," decided Ruth would be the one to treasure his mother's quilt. She has done so for more than sixty years.

Sarah Ann's Chimney Sweep quilt is a charming example of pioneer artistry. Even though many of the patches are cut from scraps of light prints and solids, the overall impression is that this quilt is made up primarily of dark, rich colors. The surprising red sashing adds to the illusion, making the quilt appear strong and solid despite the tiny squares and the even tinier muslin triangles that make up two of the squares in each four-patch block. The backing is a deep cocoa brown and white print. The quilting is done in black thread around each pieced square, with horizontal lines quilted onto the plain blocks and straight lines running along the sashing. Sarah Ann would certainly recognize her quilt today; it has been carefully kept and protected since sixteen-year-old Ruth became its keeper.

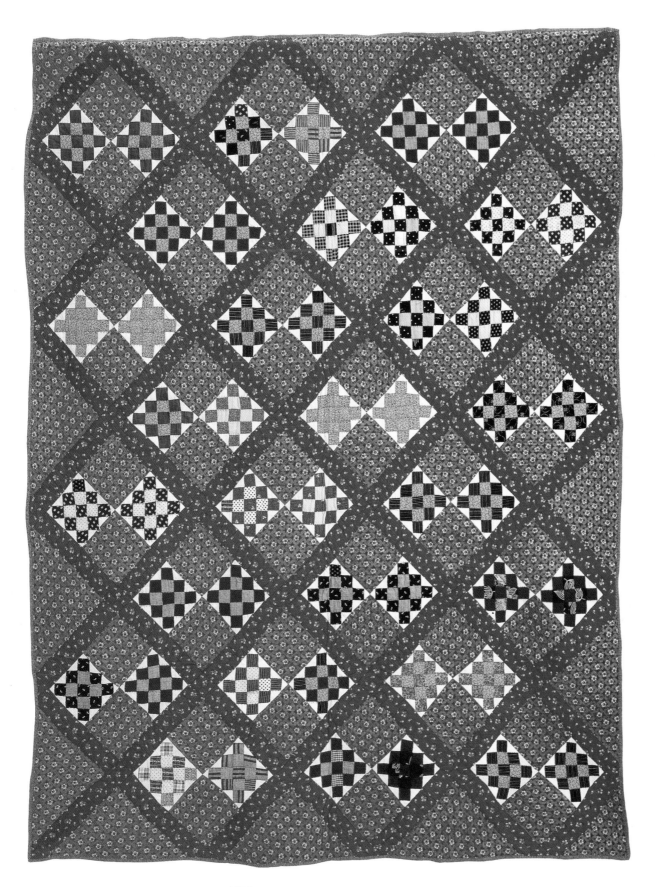

1890s

**Chimney Sweep in
a Four-patch**

65″ x 85½″

Cotton

Made by Sarah Ann Howard Laney

(1822–1902)

Made in Salt Lake City, Salt Lake County,

Utah

Owned by Ruth Harris

Chief Kanosh, leader of the Pahvant Utes, often ate at the table of Baldwin and Barbara Watts, who lived in the little Utah town named for him. Their daughter Barbara Jane remembered it clearly almost ninety years later:

> Chief Kanosh was a good chief and always preached to his people not to fight or steal from the white people. He often came to our home just at dinner time, especially on Sunday. We used to trade horses to the Indians for large sacks of pine nuts. Even today I enjoy telling the good qualities of the Indians at the Kanosh Camp.

Barbara Jane Watts was born in the northern Utah town of Huntsville in 1863. While she was still a child, her family moved hundreds of miles southward to Kanosh, Utah, where her father worked on a mountain ranch on Watts's Mountain. He was a friend of the great Chief Kanosh and spoke many of the different tribal languages. Barbara was known as "Ducky" to her family and often told her children and grandchildren the story of Ducky Spring. She had become lost in Kanosh Canyon, and when her father found her near a spring, he named it after her.

Barbara's childhood home in Kanosh was a three-room log house. The family made candles out of grease or tallow, with wicks of carpet warp, and slept on beds with ropes laced back and forth between the sides to hold the straw- or husk-filled mattresses. Pillows were stuffed with duck and chicken feathers bought from the Indians. Laundry was done on a washboard. The heavy flatiron used to smooth the wrinkles from homemade clothes had to be filled with hot coals, even on sweltering summer days. The Watts

children worked at chores most of the day, gathering sego lily bulbs and pigweed, which their mother often cooked. Mrs. Watts had the first sewing machine in town.

There was an oasis of peace and comfort for Barbara in the busy pioneer settlement: Grandma Watts. In the autobiography Barbara dictated at the age of ninety-three, she recalled her grandmother in this way:

> Grandma Watts was a beautiful, aristocratic lady, very dignified. She looked like a queen sitting in her high back rocker. We grandchildren loved to sleep in her cozy bedroom with the old fashioned stove, dresser, bed, and cedar chest in which she kept rock candy for treats.

Barbara married Jacob Hopkins in Kanosh in May 1881, and during the next fifteen years she gave birth to twelve children, including two sets of twins.

No one is certain when or why Barbara made her Diamond quilt. There are forty-eight full patchwork diamonds and forty-five plain green diamonds hand stitched together to form the quilt top. A homemade wool batting, probably from the Hopkins's sheep herd, was placed between the quilt top and the red and green print backing before Barbara quilted around the diamonds. It was a warm and useful quilt, a comforting reminder to Barbara of the pioneer days she remembered so fondly.

Late 1800s

Diamonds

65" x 94"

Cotton

Made by Barbara Jane Watts Hopkins

(1863–1959)

Made in Kanosh, Millard County, Utah

Owned by Fillmore Museum

Harriett Ambrosine Hacking lived all of her eighty-five years in Cedar Fort, Utah, a small farming community fifteen miles west of Lehi. She was born there in 1858 to John Sampson Hacking and his wife, Jane Clark, who had been childhood sweethearts and English immigrants to America, crossing the plains to Utah in 1856. Harriett's birthplace was a large, one-room adobe house built by her father, a shelter outgrown long before a larger home was completed in 1874 for the family that by then numbered eight children. Six more children were born to John and Jane Hacking for a total of fourteen; Harriett was the second child and the oldest daughter.

Harriett, who never married, was like a mother to her younger brothers and sisters, contributing uncalculated hours of labor and love to ensure that her mother's household ran smoothly. The youngest child in the family was born when Jane was forty-seven years old, and twenty-seven-year-old Harriett virtually raised the little boy as her own. She also raised the daughter of her sister Jane Elizabeth, who had died when little Alice was two years old.

Harriett often acted as a nurse and midwife to her family and the community, having received professional training at the Brigham Young Academy. Through the years, she cheerfully cooked and cleaned for her younger siblings whenever they were enrolled in school. Five of the fourteen children of John and Jane Hacking obtained an education at Brigham Young Academy.

One of Harriett's greatest talents required a needle and thread. She was a flawless seamstress, sewing both women's dresses and men's shirts, using fabrics brought by wagon from the newly organized Zion's Cooperative Mercantile Institution in Salt Lake City to her father's store in Cedar Fort. Before electricity was brought into the home, she cut and stitched by candle-light or by the flickering light of a fireplace. She also quilted, never wasting a scrap of fabric if her beautiful, slender hands could transform the nondescript shirting leftovers into something useful and warm and pretty.

Harriett created The Hand quilt primarily from shirting pieces sometime before the turn of the century. The design is hand quilted in a Baptist Fan pattern, which begins in the corner of a block and expands outward like ripples on a lake.

For quilt owner Lola Hacking Fowlke, her Aunt Hattie was a permanent and endearing part of life. Hattie and her youngest brother, Lola's father, lived as co-owners of the family home the rest of their lives. After suffering a severe stroke in 1917, Hattie was not expected to live, but she survived for nearly three decades, outliving nine of her doctors and many nurses. With great difficulty, she could walk with the aid of two canes. Even so, she never complained and never asked for special treatment. Lola's mother, Keren Hacking, cared for her untiringly with never a cross word passing between the two women. Aunt Hattie was always a needed part of the family, making quilts in her old age for her nieces and nephews and even teaching Lola's younger brother to read. She died at the age of eighty-five in 1944.

Harriett Ambrosine Hacking

Before 1900

The Hand

(A Bear Paw Variation)

76″ x 89″

Cotton

Made by Harriett Ambrosine Hacking

(1858–1944)

Made in Cedar Fort, Utah County, Utah

Owned by Lola Hacking Fowlke

Elizabeth Jackson Reid

What a sad reunion must have awaited Thomas Jackson when he met his family at Ellis Island in 1856 after a nine-month separation. He had left his wife and six children in Manchester, England, to come to America and prepare for their trip to Utah, the Mormon Zion. But when he at last embraced Alice and the children, the sorrowful story was told: the youngest child, a son, had died just before the ship landed. After a quick burial, the family joined with the Grosbeck wagon company and journeyed west.

Elizabeth Jackson was five years old when her family briefly settled in Salt Creek, Utah, later known as Nephi. They moved to Payson, where Elizabeth grew to adulthood. Because her mother's midwifery skills were in constant demand, Elizabeth took on the responsibility of cooking and caring for the younger children in the family. She was an excellent seamstress, even sewing her mother's and father's clothing. In 1869, Elizabeth married John Kirkwood Reid.

In 1875, Elizabeth and John moved to Manti, one of the oldest settlements in Utah. By the 1870s, the Indian troubles in the area had subsided and the town was a peaceful and prosperous place to live. The Reid family remained in Manti until May 1879 when they packed their belongings in a covered wagon and embarked on a ten-day journey east to a primitive and remote area known as Castle Valley.

John had traveled to Castle Valley earlier, in the fall of 1878, and built a dugout for the family to live in temporarily, but when they arrived in Castle Valley that spring, the dugout was hard to find. Wintering sheep had trampled the shelter and some repair work had to be done before John could leave for Manti to retrieve the remainder of the household goods and buy more supplies. During his absence Elizabeth and the six children had little to eat, except for some wheat which had been accidentally doused in coal oil during the rugged trip. Elizabeth cleaned the wheat as best she could and ground it in a coffee mill. It kept them alive.

Before John returned to Castle Valley, a terrifying cloudburst swept across the countryside. Soon nothing but running water surrounded the little dugout. When water rushed in the window and door of the shelter, Elizabeth quickly reacted. She placed chairs on top of the table and the bed and put the children and the family's meager belongings on top of the chairs. Then she ran out into the torrential rain to try to divert the floodwaters away from the dugout. Miraculously, a man on horseback came by and, grabbing the shovel from Elizabeth's hands, quickly changed the water's course. For hours after the storm subsided, the older children and Elizabeth bailed muck and water from their wet and muddy little home.

Elizabeth and John soon moved out of the temporary dirt shelter and eventually raised seven sons and eight daughters in a larger, more permanent home in Orangeville. Visiting with her neighbors was a challenge, but Elizabeth thought nothing of walking for miles with a new baby in her arms to visit the families scattered across the valley. She was a small woman, no more than five feet tall, but strong, energetic, and healthy. She made clothes for the entire family, weaving cloth from wool that was gathered by the children off of the plentiful sagebrush in the area through which sheep had grazed. She also made scrap quilts to fight off winter's chill.

According to Reid family history, The Courthouse Steps quilt was made primarily from the inside seams of old clothing. Most of the pieces vary in width and length, with some of the smaller pieces measuring only three-eighths of an inch in size. There is no batting, and it is quilted in a grid design. The quilt was originally inherited by Elizabeth's daughter Alice, who gave it to her own daughter Dorothy. Dorothy in turn gave it to her cousin Mary Lue, who was born two weeks after her great-grandmother Elizabeth's death in 1934. It is one of her dearest treasures along with a wooden bed she owns believed to have been built by Elizabeth's father, Thomas Jackson.

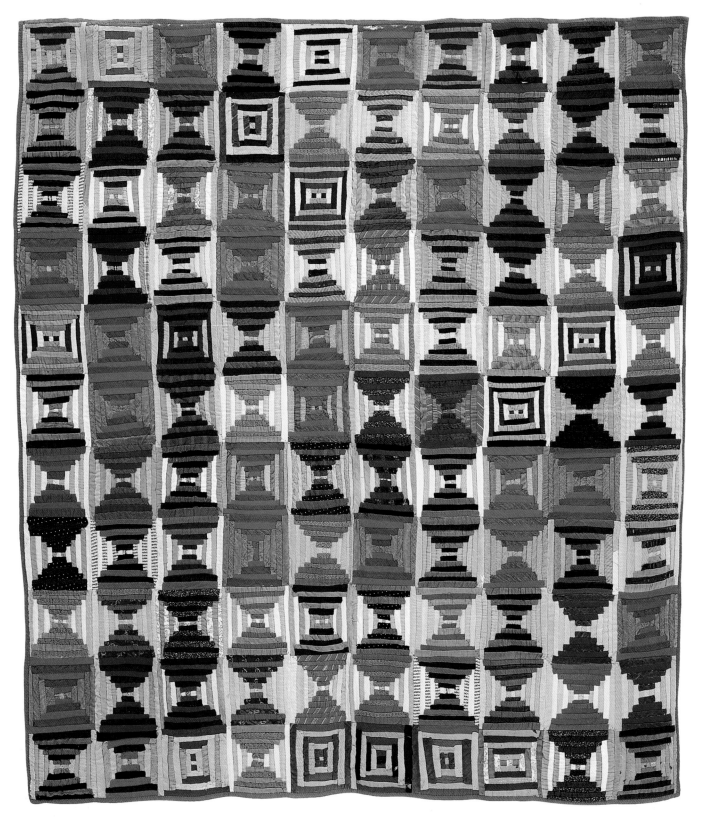

1900

**Log Cabin,
Courthouse Steps Setting**

67½" x 76"

Wool, silk, and cotton

Made by Elizabeth Jackson Reid

(1851–1934)

Made in Orangeville, Emery County, Utah

Owned by Mary Lue Gordon

Minnie
Colgrove
Ashby

Janine Rees had seen the old, Depression era quilt before, a worn, pastel nine-patch made by her great-grandmother. Originally, it had been used more for warmth than for beauty, then as a camp quilt, and most recently as not much more than a rag. Her parents had used it all winter, and perhaps for many winters past, to keep ice from forming overnight on the windshield of the car. It wasn't the quilt itself that interested Janine so much that day, but what appeared to be inside of it. Something red could be seen through the tattered, frozen fabric, something red and quiltlike.

"Mom, can I have this old quilt?" she asked, prying the stiff bundle from the front of the car and carrying it into the house to thaw. For two weeks she picked out every quilting stitch, both front and back, of the old quilt to reveal a red, black, and white quilt that had been made almost a century earlier. Her father did not recall ever seeing the quilt before, but he was certain it was made by his grandmother Minnie Colgrove Ashby. A close inspection of the quilt showed that it had been repaired in many places and that the binding had been replaced along one edge. It was worn and faded, with tufts of cotton batting visible in several spots. Too worn to use on a bed, Minnie must have decided, but still good enough to use inside a new quilt. So she placed it inside the pastel nine-patch she pieced and quilted in the 1930s, where it remained until Janine freed it in 1988.

Minnie Ashby was a devoted quilter, as much for the company of other quilters and the socializing it provided as for the needlework itself. She was a stalwart member of "The Club," a loosely organized group of friends and relatives who gathered regularly for quilting bees in the little Utah farming town of Fillmore, which was Minnie's home from the day she was born in the fall of 1872 until she died in 1948. Minnie married Nathaniel Ashby there in 1895, and together they raised four children and ran a farm. Nathaniel died suddenly in 1920 at the age of forty-two, leaving his widow burdened with their heavy debt. Minnie milked cows for many years to pay off the bills. As her children grew and married, they took care of Minnie so that she never had to go on government relief, even during the Great Depression.

Minnie was a very frugal, resourceful person. Her grandson recalls that she always kept a little extra money tucked away in her feather bed. She was also a kind and gentle person who spent most of her adult life serving her neighbors in Fillmore. One of her duties, assigned to her by the L.D.S. Relief Society, was to prepare the dead for burial. She often made burial clothes, helped prepare the bodies of the dead for burial, and sat through the long night with the family and the deceased.

Circa 1900

Shoo Fly

72" x 78"

Cotton

Made by Minnie Colgrove Ashby

(1872–1948)

Made in Fillmore, Millard County, Utah

Owned by Janine Speakman Rees

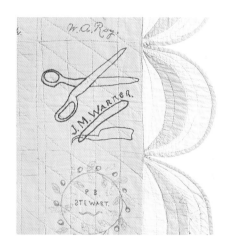

The early pioneers had little use for barbers. A bearded face was easier to maintain than a clean shaven one, and if a man needed a haircut, his wife or neighbor would oblige. Occasionally, someone would offer to provide a "professional" haircut for "two bits," but for the most part cutting hair was a necessary nuisance best left for the Saturday night before a wedding or a funeral.

As the number of towns and settlements in Utah increased, the town barber became a pleasant fixture on many main streets. The barbershop became a gathering place for men, especially in the little Mormon towns where there were no saloons or other "private" places to discuss the weather, farming conditions, politics, and business. For fifty-two years, the town of Fillmore had the same barber, a man named Francis Cannon "Can" Melville who probably cut every male head of hair and shaved or trimmed every beard in the county seat of Millard County.

Can Melville was born in Fillmore in 1860, nine years after the town's founding by thirty pioneer families led by Anson Call. Many of the people who settled in the Pahvant Valley were from the British Isles, like Can's father, Alexander Melville, from Scotland, and his mother, Jane Dutson, from England. After immigrating to Utah in the early 1850s, the couple settled in Fillmore and raised a family of ten children.

In 1885, Can started his barbershop in one corner of a shoe repair shop owned by Lafe Christopherson and John Cooper. Over the next five decades, the shop moved several times, but the clientele and Can's good nature remained constant. In 1901, the town honored him with the tan Friendship quilt that now belongs to the Fillmore Museum.

The pieced and embroidered cotton quilt is a perfect square bordered with twenty-four ornate cream and camel-colored fabric scallops. Each of the forty-nine squares that make up the quilt is embroidered with objects and names reflective of the time, the town, the people, and the barber of Fillmore. Many squares are stitched with wild-flowers, fruits, birds, and butterflies, but there are also a wine decanter and glasses, a knife and fork, fans, and a pair of scissors. All of the names embroidered on the quilt are men's names, such as Alonzo Ray, J. M. Warner, Gabriel Huntsman, and Riley Huntsman. If the town meant to pay tribute to their favorite barber with the gift of such a splendid quilt, they certainly succeeded.

The fascinating barber quilt of Can Melville now sits in the Fillmore Museum, which is housed in the former capitol building of what was Utah Territory. After the seat of state government was moved to Salt Lake City, the building was used variously as a civic center, church, school, theater, and jail. In the 1920s, the Daughters of Utah Pioneers proposed that the building be restored and used as a museum, and it was eventually placed in the custodial care of the D.U.P. In 1957, it became a state park.

1901

Friendship Quilt

78" x 78"

Cotton

Makers unknown

Made in Fillmore, Millard County, Utah

Owned by Fillmore Museum

Jane
Walker
Smith

"I well remember when I was a little girl, my father was moving from Vermont to Nauvoo with his family of ten children and my mother, a brave, delicate woman." So begins the brief personal history written by Jane Walker Smith, born in Peacham, Vermont, on August 2, 1832. She continues her recollections, telling of the massacre of Latter-day Saints at Haun's Mill, Missouri, on October 30, 1838, and the wounding of her father, John Walker, who was shot through the right arm as the bullets flew "like hailstones." As the family waited for news about him, a young man came running into the camp telling the women to flee into the woods or they would all share the same fate as the Saints killed at the mill. Jane's mother, Lydia Holmes Walker, told her children that the Lord could take care of them just as well in their wagons as in the woods, and they stayed where they were. In the morning, the camp was surrounded by a mob.

Jane continues: "They searched the wagons, took the guns and ammunition and threatened to kill every one, little and big. A woman came with the mob. I can see her now with her knee on a chair. She looked at us and said, 'I would like to see every one killed big and small.' I thought, 'What a wicked woman you are.' They finally ordered us to move on. We were just ready to eat breakfast so we had to go without. The mob followed us until noon. We had to face rain and sleet, so the mob did not enjoy the ride. They ordered us off the main road and said if we were seen again they would kill every one. We camped in the woods that night, could not make a fire for fear of being seen. We had to make the beds on the ground

with nothing but the canopy of heaven to shelter us, and were cold and hungry."

John Walker finally met up with his family, and they made their way to Nauvoo, Illinois. The children were ill for six months and John was very sick; Lydia died in January 1842. Jane lived for a time with Prophet Joseph Smith and his family in Nauvoo before his death in 1844. At the age of sixteen, she came to Utah with her sister Lucy Kimball in the Heber C. Kimball Company of emigrants. She entered the Salt Lake Valley driving a yoke of oxen down what is now known as Emigration Canyon.

Jane married Lot Smith in Salt Lake City on Valentine's Day 1852, the second of his eight wives. They moved to a large, rock house in Farmington, where eight children were born to them, six daughters and two sons, all of them living to maturity. Jane was an ardent worker and a good neighbor, known to her friends in later years as "Aunt Jane."

Jane worked daily at all the chores required in a pioneer household: the cooking, cleaning, washing, gardening, sewing, quilting, and a hundred others. To all these, she added one more job: she grew silkworms, taking advantage of the numerous mulberry trees that grew along Main Street in Farmington. Silkworms will eat only mulberry leaves, finely chopped and sprinkled over the top of the tiny worms. For twenty to thirty days, Jane would change the papers underneath the worms and add more and more leaves, which the worms ate and ate, growing to over three inches in length and shedding their skins four times. When they were ready to begin spinning their cocoons, the worms stopped eating and started moving their heads slowly back and forth. At that point, Jane would provide little twigs or

straw on which the worms could attach their cocoons of spun silk threads. Three days later, she would unwind the silk threads onto spools. From the thread she would weave fabric for the silk dresses women so greatly admired but had difficulty finding. Aunt Jane grew silkworms until she was nearly eighty years old.

Jane Walker Smith stitched her delicate pink and white quilt when she was seventy-two years old. It is not as fragile as it appears. Like Jane, it weathered trials and disasters, most notably the flood of August 13, 1923, in Farmington, Utah. Jane's daughter Annetta Smith Udy inherited the quilt following her mother's death and kept it in her bedroom. When the rains flooded Farmington, Annetta's bedroom was washed away and the quilt went with it. She later found it caught on a tree stump. The fate of the bedroom, however, was never determined.

1904

Pink and White Triangles

68″ x 76″

Cotton

Made by Jane Walker Smith (1832–1912)

Made in Farmington, Davis County, Utah

Owned by Bernice Earl

Sarah
Elizabeth
Crook
Carlile

The striking feature of this Log Cabin quilt is the arrangement of the blocks on point, creating horizontal straight furrows rather than the typical diagonal alignment. Highlighting the unusual placement of the squares is the bright blue fabric that shines in many of the blocks, giving an electric aspect to the otherwise dark and serious quilt. There does not appear to be batting in the quilt, although the pieces are quilted around the outside of the block and the center square, or "hearth." Owner Karen Springer thinks the quilt may be filled with feathers, rather than cotton or wool.

Karen's great-grandmother Sarah Elizabeth Crook created this uncommonly beautiful quilt in her lifelong home of Heber City, Utah. Sarah was the first pioneer child born in the fort in the Heber Valley following the first harvest there in 1859. The settlers wintered in Utah Valley and returned the next year to Heber Valley to build permanent homes, many using locally quarried red sandstone. All material goods were scarce during those years. With one pair of shoes shared between Sarah and her brother John, they took turns using the shoes for social events and dances; it was understood that when one of them was wearing the shoes, the other one stayed home.

In 1878, Sarah married John Carlile in the L.D.S. Endowment House in Salt Lake City, a day-and-a-half trip by horse and wagon. Upon their return to Heber, the couple moved into a little log house, where six of their ten children were born. Later, they moved into a rock house paid for with a team of horses.

Sarah's husband John died in 1902 after twenty-four years of marriage. Their eight living children ranged in age from three to twenty-one. Sarah filled her days with serving others—caring for the sick and needy, making burial clothes for the dead, and feeding the hungry. She also took in washing, made quilts, grew a garden that produced enough surplus vegetables to sell to her neighbors, and often worked as a midwife. The people of Heber City knew her as "Aunt Sarah." Many times she was called upon in the dark of night to minister to the sick or to quiet a crying baby.

Two of the grandest times for Sarah's children centered on the town parades on the Fourth of July and on Pioneer Day, July 24. The Carliles were well known for their six white horses that were a regular feature of the parades. The boys would carefully scrub the horses' coats and braid their tails and manes, then place a blanket on each horse to keep it clean for the day's events. Inside the house, Sarah and her daughters made paper pompoms of red, white, and blue, to be placed on either side of the horses' bridles, emphasizing the beautiful white heads held so proudly and so high.

In August 1994, Sarah's grandchildren held a "cousin's party" to share information about their grandmother. They reminisced about the constant quilting that went on in Sarah's house, often with a whole quilt being finished in one day. They loved to get underneath a quilt on a frame and cause the quilters to prick their fingers, receiving a thump on the head with a thimbled finger as a reward. Sarah is remembered by her descendants as a friendly and loving woman who made friends, neighbors, and even strangers feel like a part of the family.

1908

Log Cabin, Straight Furrows Setting

77" x 78"

Cotton, silk, and wool

Made by Sarah Elizabeth Crook Carlile

(1859–1919)

Made in Heber City, Wasatch County, Utah

Owned by Karen Springer

Keren Bingham Hacking

Keren Bingham Hacking's fingers were often raw from the unavoidable needle pricks that accompany long hours at the quilting frame. She worked through the spring and summer months to repair old quilts and make new ones, knowing that the thick, wool quilts would soon become as essential to her family as good food and a warm fire. Of the six bedrooms in the family home, four were in the unheated upstairs; more than one quilt was required to keep a shivering child warm through the frigid winter nights. Keren and her husband, Will, had six children to insulate from bitter winds and blizzards, so she worked tirelessly in preparation, usually using a nine-patch pattern with sashing between the blocks and outing flannel on the quilt back.

Keren had learned to quilt as a young girl, probably from her mother, Margarett Louisa Gfroerer Bingham. Louisa was the second wife of Thomas Bingham, Jr.; her identical twin sister Mary Elizabeth was his first wife. Thomas had fallen in love with Louisa and asked for her hand in marriage, but her father declined, stating that since Mary Elizabeth had been born first, she would have to be married first. Thomas married her in June of 1874 and married Louisa sixteen months later.

The fifth of six children born to her mother and father, Keren grew up in Maeser, three miles west of Vernal, Utah, living in one of the two large log houses Thomas built for his wives. Keren's mother was in charge of doing the sewing, washing, and ironing for the family, and her aunt Mary Elizabeth was the cook. Keren and her brothers and sisters walked two miles each way to grade school, especially enjoying the winter when they could walk through the fields over the tops of the fences on the deep and crusty snow. Keren completed the eighth grade in Maeser, then advanced to the Uintah Stake Academy in Vernal, which she attended from 1905 to 1907. When she was twenty-two, Keren went to Brigham Young University in Provo, Utah, with her half-sister Edna. It was there that she dated and eventually became engaged to Thomas William "Will" Hacking of Cedar Fort.

Keren spent the summer months of 1912 with her family in Maeser making wedding plans and preparing for her move to Cedar Fort, where the couple would live with Will's parents. She made her wedding dress and finished the Cherry Basket quilt as part of her wedding trousseau. Her friends had pieced the squares, which she sewed together then quilted with the help of those same friends. Keren pieced the back from shirt and dress scraps, creating a stylish, well-balanced design from varied sizes and shapes of primarily blue and brown shirting. The back is brought to the front for a charming edging.

Will came by buggy for Keren the first week of October. His oldest brother, Jim, and Jim's wife, Annie, came along as chaperones. The foursome planned to travel first to Cedar Fort to drop off Keren's belongings, then on to Salt Lake City, where Keren and Will would be married in the L.D.S. Temple. It was a trip that should have taken eight days at the most, but inclement weather forced them to remain at Cedar Fort for two weeks before they were able to travel to Salt Lake City and be married at last on October 16, 1912. Keren was the last daughter-in-law to join the large Hacking family.

Keren's daughter, Lola Fowlke, remembers her mother as a quiet, unassuming woman who graciously filled her role as the Hacking family hostess. Family members were always visiting the large home at Cedar Fort, and Keren cooked their meals on a wood-burning stove, washed piles of dirty dishes, and made up extra beds with fresh linens. She also selflessly cared for her husband's sister, Aunt Hattie, for twenty-seven years following a debilitating stroke. Keren would be pleased to know that today her daughter Lola owns the house at Cedar Fort, and has spent many years restoring it inside and out to its former glory.

1912

Cherry Basket

82″ x 69″

Cotton

Made by Keren Bingham Hacking

(1888–1977)

Made in Maeser (Vernal), Uintah County,

Utah

Owned by Lola Fowlke

Reverse side of quilt

Birdie Adams spread the newly finished quilt top across her bed to check for any noticeable flaws. She had spent months embroidering the velvet, satin, and silk hearth pieces in the centers of the blocks with flowers—mostly pansies that reminded her of her mother's garden—and the initials of the members of her family: D. A. for her brother Del; F. A. for Frank. There was one block with a butterfly, another with brown cattails, and one with an anchor. The top was ready to finish now, but Birdie would not quilt it like every other log cabin she had ever seen. This quilt would be tied with red ribbons to match the backing. And there would be no batting either, for this was a quilt to treasure and display—not a useful, heavy quilt to keep her warm, but a keepsake of her approaching marriage.

Bird Belinda Adams was already an accomplished seamstress and musician when she married Harold Layton at the age of sixteen. She had studied piano at the McCune School of Music in Salt Lake City. She loved to read about history, and she often played the piano to soothe the two daughters and two sons she had with Harold. The little family moved to California for one year while Harold worked in the nut fields, then returning to Utah. In 1929, Birdie and Harold divorced.

A divorced, single woman was not an easy thing to be at the height of the Great Depression, but Birdie made the most of her numerous talents in her determination to survive. She taught piano lessons and accompanied high school music students who were preparing for concerts or competitions. Somehow, she found the money to attend Gray's Beauty School in Ogden, Utah, and eventually opened a beauty shop, which she called Birdie's Beauty Salon. She sewed clothes for her children and continued to fill the home with music. Lorraine remembers her older brother Hyrum coming in from hoeing beets and saying, "My back hurts; if you'll just play me a tune, it will feel better."

Birdie married Lloyd Udy in 1940 and moved with him to Rockland, Idaho. During World War II she sewed clothes for the war effort, always tucking something extra, like a bar of soap, into one of the pockets. She also did aerial observations in Idaho, watching for enemy aircraft. Before she left for Idaho, Birdie gave her daughter Lorraine the Log Cabin wedding quilt, the only quilt remaining of the many quilts she had made.

Birdie returned to Utah in 1972 and lived there until her death at the age of ninety.

Bird
Belinda
Adams
Layton

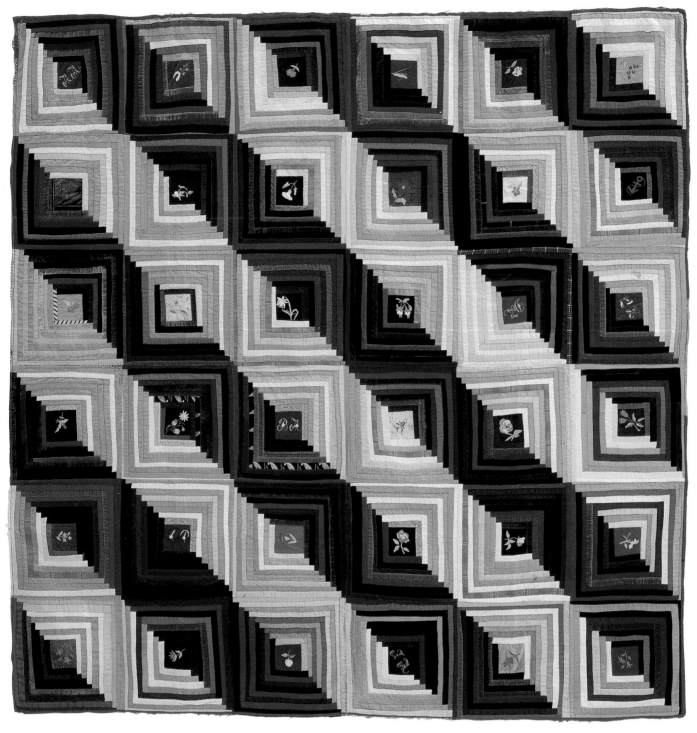

1912

**Log Cabin,
Straight Furrows Setting**

72" x 73"

Cotton and silk

Made by Bird Belinda Adams Layton

(1896–1986)

Made in Layton, Davis County, Utah

Owned by Lorraine Layton Jacobson

The Crazy Quilt began as a humble bedcover stitched by colonial women who had saved woolen scraps from their family's worn-out clothing in hopes that something useful and warm could be made from them. The fabric pieces were randomly sewn together "crazy fashion" with a back and padding added, the entire assemblage fastened together with colorful yarn knots. Although useful and warm, the quilt was not especially beautiful and was generally relegated to the back bedroom. By the close of the nineteenth century, however, the Crazy Quilt had matured into an exquisite "couch throw" or "slumber robe" to be on display in the parlor, a textile celebration fashioned from elaborately embroidered and hand-painted silk and velvet patches. What began as a haphazard joining of scraps for the sake of frugality gradually evolved into an art form.

The Vests Crazy Quilt created by Emma Jean Liston in 1913 is an original and unusual representation of the Victorian art of patchwork. Using discarded men's vests—the fronts only—she made a quilt top that looks as much like an unfinished puzzle as it does a bedcover. Arranged sideways and upside down, the vest fronts begin to take on the appearance of puzzle pieces in search of a mate. It is fascinating to try to match the two sides of each vest, but difficult to do so without being distracted by the beautiful herringbone stitches that sew each piece to the whole. And the variety of vests! The quilt is a visual history lesson in the style and construction of one of the most common articles of men's clothing in the early twentieth century.

Some of the vests are thought to have belonged to Emma Jean's husband, Perry Martindale Liston, or they might have been worn by her sons or neighbors. Her youngest daughter, who owns the quilt, says she probably just "gathered vests up" until she had enough. At that time, any man who wore a suit, wore a vest. Whether to speed along the quilt's construction or simply to save clothing that had some sentimental value to her, how unique it was for Emma to use the entire vest front, rather than cutting it into smaller pieces. The effect is unforgettable.

During the winter the Vests quilt was made, Emma was living in Beaver, Utah, with three of her older children so they could attend school, probably at the Murdock Academy established there by the L.D.S. church in 1898. Perry remained at home in Escalante, Utah, with the other children, although it was not uncommon for the entire family to live on the ranch in the summertime and spend the winter in the city. Living with Emma was Auntie DeVoe, a member of the family for thirty years. She probably helped piece, quilt, and embroider the Vests quilt. With such a heavy wool top and the homemade wool batting and wool back, it was difficult for the women to take more than three stitches per inch.

Emma Jean Shirts was born in Manti, Utah, to early pioneer settlers Mary Adeline Lee and Don Carlos Shirts. She married Perry Liston of Little Keg Creek, Iowa, in 1876. Perry was eleven years her senior and had first met her when she was a little girl, waiting until shortly after her fifteenth birthday to marry her. The two were early settlers in Escalante, impressed by the mild climate and abundant grazing land where the grass was so tall that a reclining cow was invisible. Ten children were born to Emma Jean and Perry in Escalante, one son dying in infancy. Orilla is their only living child and will someday bequeath her one-of-a-kind quilt to one of her daughters for safekeeping.

1913

Crazy Quilt: Vests

72″ x 86″

Miscellaneous fabrics including wool,
velvet, men's suiting

Made by Emma Jean Shirts Liston

(1861–1933)

Made in Beaver, Beaver County, Utah

Owned by Orilla Cowles

Denmark is a country that does not have abundant natural resources: no coal, iron, petroleum, mineral deposits, mountains, or large forests. It does have, however, two things that have helped make it one of the most prosperous nations in Europe: abundant farmland and frugal, energetic people. Centuries of life on this peninsula and its surrounding islands have taught the Danish people that to be successful one must work hard and live moderately.

Peter Christian and Celia Johanna Petersen were born in beautiful Denmark in the middle of the nineteenth century, Peter in 1847 and Johanna in 1851. Peter left the city of Aalborg to find work in the country, and there he met and married Johanna. They returned to Peter's hometown, where their first two children were born, each dying in infancy. A daughter, Christina (Stena), was born next, followed by Hyrum and Mena. The family lived in a little thatched-roof house with a clay floor. There was a pond nearby, and the countryside was splendidly green. From her front door, Johanna could see the ships sailing on the ocean. Peter worked in town, walking the five miles to and from his job each day.

The Petersens worked hard. Both husband and wife sheared sheep. Johanna washed and carded the wool, spun yarn, and wove it into cloth. She then sent the finished cloth to be professionally pressed before she cut and stitched it into clothes. She was an excellent seamstress, quilter, and hat maker.

When Stena was eight years old, Johanna and Peter joined the L.D.S. church. A missionary from Ephraim, Utah, loaned them a small amount of money, and they made preparations to sail to America. They decided Peter and their five-year-old son, Hyrum, would

go first to find a home and a job before the rest of the family followed. In 1884, Johanna stood at the door with her new baby, Elsa, watching her husband and little son sail away, straining her eyes to see the white handkerchief Peter waved as the ship left Denmark.

Peter found work in Ephraim, Utah, herding sheep for fifteen dollars a month, and three months later, the family was reunited. Johanna, with her three daughters, had experienced a hard, stormy journey: she told Peter how seasick and miserable they all had been. All her dishes were broken, either from the storm or rough handling. Stena recalled years later that "when we got to New York . . . everything looked so funny—clothes were funny, wagons were different, and people talked so funny and everything was so big and strange."

The family lived in a one-room house in Ephraim for eight years. Peter never earned more than twenty-five dollars a month, but Johanna and the children helped in every way they could. Johanna continued to earn money with her sewing, making pillows, velvet handbags and bonnets, hats, coats, capes, and, of course, quilts. She sold one of the quilts for an amazing three dollars.

A diphtheria epidemic in Ephraim brought sorrow to the Petersen family when five-year-old Elsa died after just a few hours of illness. Because the disease was highly contagious, no one was allowed to enter the home except Johanna, who had to dress and lay out the body of her child. The next day, a man who had survived the disease helped Peter bury his daughter. Hyrum had been across the river when the family was stricken, and stayed with neighbors until the danger of exposure had passed.

When their oldest child was sixteen, Peter and Johanna moved the family to Manti, Utah. Peter bought five acres of ground and built a new house and barn. They raised cows, chickens, and pigs. Johanna became known for her kind acts of service to the lonely and the sick. On many cold winter nights, she carried a pail of hot soup to an older couple who needed help in caring for themselves. In the morning, she would leave home early to go make their fires for them. Johanna died in Manti two years after she made the quilt that was given to her granddaughter Ruth on her wedding day.

The puffs are squares of fabric, gathered along the edges and lightly stuffed with wool before being sewn together. The puffy sixteen-patch blocks have a three dimensional quality that makes the urge to touch them irresistible. The quilt was constructed from six strips of blocks and sashing sewn together. The dark green and purple border was then added, and the outline of the blocks was quilted and backstitched with black thread. Johanna tied the quilt with white cotton crochet thread at the corners of the maroon and green squares. The quilt was finished by folding in the top and backing and blind stitching them together.

Celia
Johanna
Christensen
Petersen

1918

Wool Biscuit Quilt

68" x 77"

Cotton

Made by Celia Johanna Christensen
Petersen (1851–1920)

Made in Manti, Sanpete County, Utah

Owned by Dorothy Stoddard

Julia Clausen made this quilt for her wedding in 1918. The pattern has been used thousands of times for thousands of brides, but few could surpass this delicate, exquisite example. No large, sweeping circles with bold colors for Julia! The dainty rings measure only nine inches in diameter, 132 of them hand pieced from pastel floral fabrics and quilted with ten very tiny, very even stitches to the inch. There is a magical, almost fairylike quality to this quilt, which was nearly lost forever when it was thrown into the trash to be discarded.

Julia died of cancer in 1966, leaving no children and very few material belongings. To her dear friend Ella Cole she had bequeathed her house and her meager possessions, including the Double Wedding Ring quilt, which was stored in a trunk. Many years later when Ella, no longer able to care for herself, was moved into a nursing home, Ella's children began sorting through her things and came upon Julia's treasure trunk with several quilts inside. Somehow it was decided the old quilts were of no value and out they went with the trash.

Ella's daughter-in-law Cally became more and more upset the more she thought about discarding the quilts. During the night, she urged her husband, Stan, Ella's oldest son, to go back to the house and retrieve at least one of the quilts.

The Clausen and Cole families met long ago when the men were working in the Bingham Copper Mine. Julia and Henry Clausen were childless and nearly old enough to be parents to the Coles. They opened their hearts and their Magna, Utah, home to the young couple, inviting them to live in the back bedroom until they could find a place of their own. Ella's first child was born in the Clausen home. When Stan was four years old, the family moved to Midvale, Utah, but kept in close touch with their old friends in Magna, whom Stan and his two brothers and sister called "Aunt Julia" and "Uncle Henry."

Stan remembers Aunt Julia as a tall, refined woman with black hair long enough to sit on. When he was a little boy he would watch her wind her hair around and around her head in the way she traditionally wore it. Thanksgiving was always spent with the Clausens. Julia, in turn, visited her adopted family several times a year in Salem, Utah, where the Coles had moved. She would ride the train, bringing bags of oranges and bananas and so much luggage the children had to be recruited to carry her things from the train station.

Julia's quilt is now safe from harm, her memory honored through admiration and respect for her skillful handiwork.

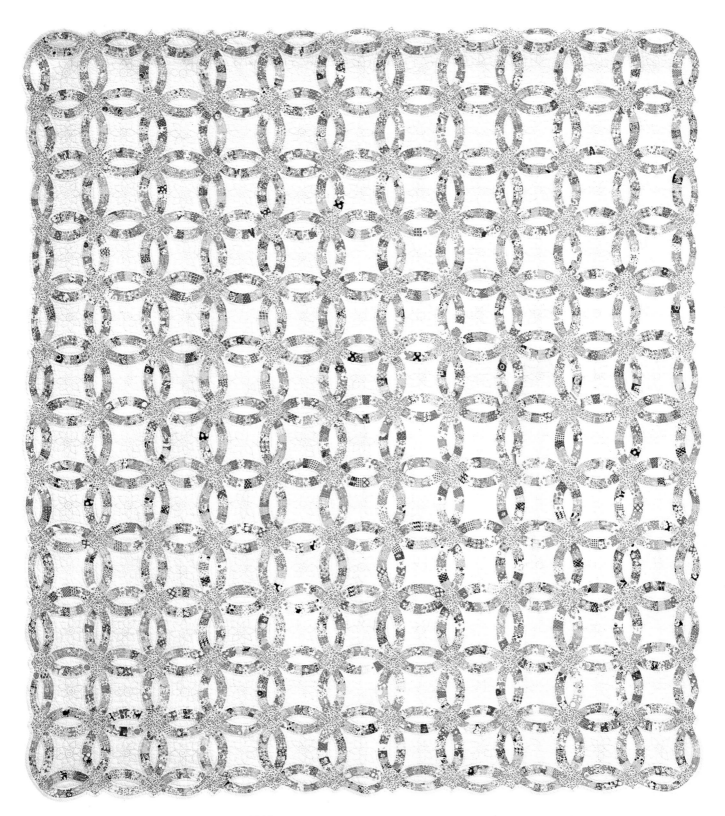

1918

Double Wedding Ring

70" x 77"

Cotton

Made by Julia Ann Gilbert Clausen

(1883–1966)

Made in Magna, Salt Lake County, Utah

Owned by Lesli Cole

Merle
Snyder
Foote

■ ■
■

Table rugs first appeared in North American folk art in the early 1800s. Although called "rugs," the textile creations were purely decorative, to be used on tabletops and dressers and never to be walked on. In the 1830s, the word *rug* or *rugg* usually referred to heavy woolen bedcovers, often decorated with flowers or figures; the table rug was simply a smaller version of the bed rug. Some table rugs had intricate designs covering the entire rug, others were constructed like an album quilt, with each block boasting its own appliqued pattern.

As families ventured westward, frugality became a major concern and the rugs began to exhibit smaller, more geometric shapes as the women sought to use their precious wool scraps. In the years following the Civil War, the rugs came to be known as "penny rugs," "dollar rugs," or "button rugs" after the items used as patterns for the small, stacked circles. The early 1900s saw a renewed interest in the quaint craft, although many of the twentieth-century rug designs were too pretentious and elaborate to be considered true reproductions of the craft.

Constructing a Penny Rug was a simple procedure that involved cutting wool circles of decreasing size and stacking and blanket stitching them together, then arranging and blanket stitching the stack onto a background of cotton, wool, or linen. Some rugs had a blanket stitched, tongue-shaped border, which was especially popular during the Victorian era. The most commonly used colors were mustards, dark greens, and all shades of red.

Merle Snyder Foote's Penny Rug was probably made in the 1920s, although its hexagonal shape was very popular in the 1890s. The unusual scalloped border sets this rug apart from most others, which commonly had straight edges or an added "tongue" border. Each of the circle stacks in this rug begins with a gray circle. On the outside edges, a smaller red circle has been blanket-stitched on. Inside the star shape, a light blue, green, or yellow circle is sewn onto the gray circles, with a smaller circle of dark blue, green, or red attached. The outside edge of the rug is stitched in white. Merle's daughter Earlene never saw the rug on the floor; it was always used as a cover on a small table.

The early 1900s were a busy time for Merle. She graduated from high school at Brigham Young University in 1913 and finished education classes a year later. In 1914, at the age of twenty-one, she began teaching fifth grade and art in Moroni, Utah. She earned sixty dollars a month.

In 1917, after previously turning down his marriage proposal and returning the diamond ring, Merle married Earl Foote in the Manti L.D.S. Temple. By 1921, they had three sons, and were living in a new brick house in Provo, Utah. Nine years later, their only daughter, Earlene, was born. Merle was a talented and well-known artist in Utah County. She won many awards for her watercolors and oil paintings, especially in her later years; she also painted china. In 1974, at the age of eighty-one, she published a history of the Pleasant View area. Merle lived to be ninety-four years old.

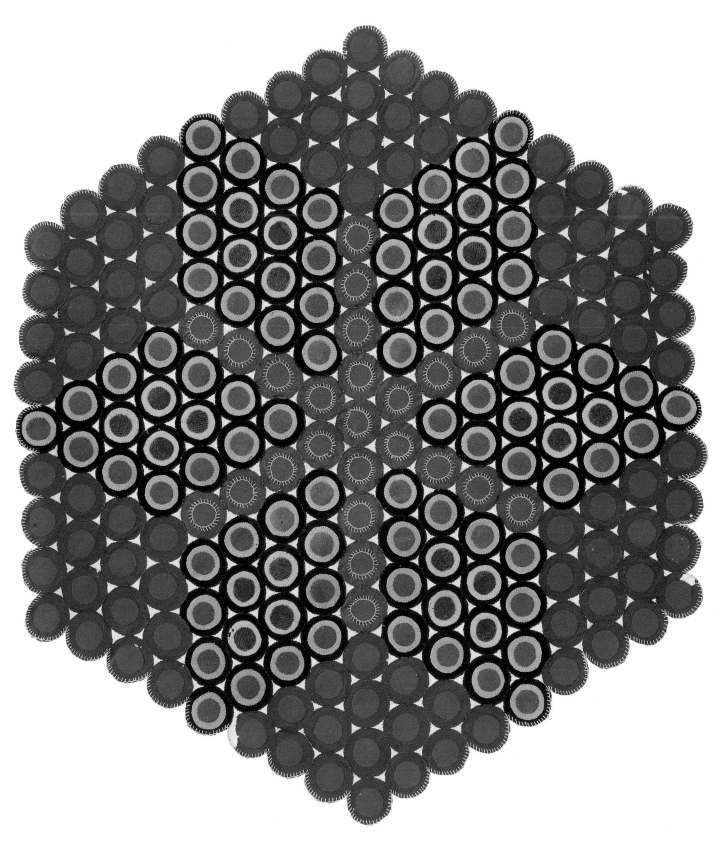

1920s

Penny Rug

40″ x 45″

Cotton and Wool

Made by Merle Snyder Foote

(1893–1988)

Made in Provo, Utah County, Utah

Owned by Earlene Foote Spencer

■ ■

Ruth
Coon
Allen

Paula Stuart was only six years old when her Grandma Allen died, but she remembers her well. Ruth Allen had doted on the granddaughter who looked so much like the daughter she had lost to a liver ailment thirty years earlier. They had the same blond hair, the same bright eyes, and identical dimpled smiles. Paula seldom got in trouble for running around or under the quilting frame that was a permanent fixture in her grandmother's dining room. Ruth had designed the frame with hinges at three-foot intervals, making it easy to fold it and the quilt out of the way when necessary. The frame required no bulky stands, fitting instead over the tops of the dining room chairs. Holes were drilled every few inches in the frame so she could tie the quilt top and backing right to the frame by stitching string through the fabric and looping the string in and out of the holes. The chairs Ruth used to hold her frame are still in the family, but the frame itself was chopped up and burned as firewood many years ago.

Ruth Allen made dozens of quilts during her lifetime. Paula owns a few of them, with the rest belonging to other family members. Once or twice Ruth might have sold a quilt, but most of them were made for her children and grandchildren. Although she owned a White treadle sewing machine, most of her quilts were sewn by hand. Some of her favorite patterns were the Double Wedding Ring, Grandmother's Flower Garden, Dresden Plate, Sunbonnet Girl, and the Lozenge design, which the family calls Wool Patchwork. It is an unusual pattern that may be a squared-off variation of the six-sided Honeycomb design. The Lozenge quilt owned by Paula was made in the 1920s, a time of great difficulty for many rural families like the Allen family and

especially for Ruth, who had lost her daughter Arva in 1922 and a two-year-old son to drowning in 1920.

Ruth was the third child of seven born to Ellen Dearden and David Franklin Coon. When Ruth was a year old, her father was badly injured in a threshing accident, losing three fingers down to the wrist. The family moved from Hunter in Salt Lake County to Huntsville in Weber County, where her father could do farming that didn't require a thresher. Ruth lived in the little farming community for the remainder of her life, marrying Alanson David Allen in 1916 and bearing eight children.

Alanson worked as a government trapper and sheepherder in Weber County. He trapped coyotes, turning in the animal's feet as proof of the kill and keeping the pelt as part of his payment. Consequently, Ruth spent many weeks at a time as the only parent in the home. Her quilting helped see her through the long hours when Alanson was herding sheep on Little Mountain in the winter and above Red Rock Ranch in the summer.

Ruth died in 1958 at the age of sixty-four. Her family gratefully remembers her love and her quilts, which have provided them with "many warm nights, wonderful picnics, and stories."

1920s

Lozenge

65" x 78"

Wool

Made by Ruth Coon Allen

(1893–1958)

Made in Huntsville, Weber County, Utah

Owned by Paula Stuart

When Ellen Matilda Busby was born in Salt Lake City in 1860, it was still the self-sufficient, homogeneous society its pioneer founders had envisioned. Mormonism was a part of everything, blurring the line between the secular and the religious. It was a cohesive, unified city, a safe place for its long-persecuted founders to live and flourish in peace. But the singular quality of the town began to change in 1869 with the coming of the railroad. By the time Ellen was twenty years old and preparing for her marriage to William Andrew Luke, Salt Lake was becoming an increasingly diversified place. Ellen's father, John Busby, was the conductor and driver of the first mule streetcar in Salt Lake City, public transport that would soon be replaced by an electric streetcar system serving 10,000 people a day. By 1890, half of the city's 45,000 residents would be non-Mormons, called "Gentiles." The speed of progress must have been staggering to the young pioneer girl. Born into a world of wagons and candlelight, she lived to see the invention of automobiles, airplanes, and the atomic bomb.

Ellen and William married on January 27, 1881, in Salt Lake City and made their home in Heber City, Utah, where William had lived since infancy. His father, Henry Luke, had built the first house outside the Heber Fort in 1860. William had been left fatherless at the age of six, and as the oldest of the six Luke children, he assumed much of the responsibility for the family as he grew older. He worked as a freighter, a road supervisor, and a farmer. In 1888 William and Ellen bought a natural hot springs in Midway, four miles north-west of Heber, which they built into Luke's Hot Pots. There were swimming pools and a hot bath heated by the natural springs, a dining room, dance hall, hotel, cabins, and a picnic area. People traveled great distances to enjoy the natural hot mineral water they believed would ease their suffering from arthritis and other illnesses. It was a resort for some, a cure for others. Mary Jane Wood, the quilt owner, remembers her grandmother Cordelia Shelton Luke bringing worn-out, no longer mendable wool swimsuits home from the Hot Pots to cut them up into quilt squares. Luke's Hot Pots was a family business until 1957, when it was sold to the Payne family and renamed The Mountain Spa.

Mary Jane was given the Bride's Nosegay quilt when she married in 1965. It had originally been given to her uncle Delbert Luke by his grandmother Ellen Busby Luke, Mary Jane's great-grandmother. Delbert had never married, so he felt that the quilt should be given to the first niece to marry. Mary Jane has treasured it for more than thirty years.

She is uncertain about the exact date it was made, but the scrapbag fabrics are vintage 1930 or earlier. Ellen's only daughter, Nellie May, helped cut the pieces. Each block has a hand-pieced, six-pointed nosegay on a light or dark plain pink background. The handle of the bouquet is of either a light or dark Nile green fabric. An interesting feature of the pattern is the small square piece placed in the angle formed where each diamond-shaped piece meets another, five per nosegay. It is hand quilted around the pieced shapes with four to six stitches per inch.

Ellen
Matilda
Busby
Luke

1920–1930

Bride's Nosegay

73" x 80"

Cotton

Made by Ellen Matilda Busby Luke

(1860–1946)

Made in Midway, Wasatch County, Utah

Owned by Mary Jane Luke Wood

Mary
Elizabeth
Jennings
Gledhill

When Brigham Young saw the brilliant red mountain near one of the newest Utah settlements in Sevier County, he suggested that the settlers rename their town. Few would have protested a name change, considering that the community had gone by the name of Neversweat since its establishment in 1874, a tongue-in-cheek name adopted in recognition of the stifling midsummer humidity and heat. So, on October 8, 1876, Neversweat became Vermilion, a more fitting name for the beautiful little farming town that had grown along the west bank of the Sevier River, ten miles northeast of Richfield.

Vermilion, Utah, was Mamie Gledhill's home for more than fifty years, from the day she was married there at the age of seventeen until her death at seventy-four. She was christened Mary Elizabeth Jennings, but always went by the name of Mamie, even signing some documents with her nickname. Born in Levan, Utah, on May 11, 1887, Mamie was the fifth of ten children born to Ane Margrethe Rasmussen and Alexander Jennings. When her parents divorced, Mamie and the other children soon learned the difficulty and the necessity of hard work.

Mamie met Hugh Lafayette Gledhill—better known as "Lafe"—at a dance in her hometown, and married him three days after Christmas in 1904. They settled on Lafe's farm in Vermilion. Six children were born to the couple, with five living to adulthood. When he was thirty-seven, Lafe was killed, crushed by a team of horses that bolted as he was hitching them to a wagon. Mamie was suddenly a widow with five children to feed and clothe and a farm to manage.

Hard work was nothing new to Mamie and she pitched right in, finding work at the gypsum plant in Sigurd, a five-mile walk from her home. Gypsum is a common mineral, calcium sulfate, and the main ingredient in plaster of paris. Today it is used to make plasterboard for the building trade. Day after day, Mamie repaired gypsum sacks, damaged from use, at the rate of one penny per finished bag. On a very good day, she could mend four hundred bags. Mamie also served as midwife for the women of Vermilion, helping her neighbors bring their infants into the world. She was also the town barber, charging twenty-five cents for a haircut.

Vermilion was a town where neighbor helped neighbor to survive. In the spring, neighbors would give tallow from butchered livestock to Mamie, who would make it into soap and then share it with the neighbors. Mamie made delicious headcheese, too, from the requisite parts of a pig her neighbors would bring her so all could share the delicacy. Good neighbors also gave her scraps of fabric which she would dye, tear into strips, roll into balls, and braid into sturdy rugs. Smaller fabric pieces were saved for the warm quilts Mamie routinely made for her family, such as the Brick quilt her granddaughter Maxine Roundy inherited after Mamie's death.

Maxine describes her grandmother as being "like a little motor," never stopping, her hands always busy. If she wasn't cleaning, she was cooking, or quilting, or crocheting, or doing anything she could think of to make life more pleasant for the people she loved.

Mamie was an anchor to ten-year-old Maxine after the death of her mother, Mamie's daughter. At the time, Mamie supported herself as a live-in maid, cleaning and cooking for her employers, and she was unable to keep Maxine with her. But Maxine always felt a great love through the letters she received from her Grandma Gledhill and from the reception she received every time she visited. Mamie would dash out of the house, arms waving, lavishing hugs and kisses and love on her precious granddaughter. According to Maxine, her grandmother was capable of a love that drew people to her like a magnet. She was also generous to a fault; Maxine had to be careful about saying she liked something her grandmother had made or she would find it tucked inside her suitcase or hidden in the car the next day.

Mamie Gledhill used ingenuity and cheerfulness to make survival an art form. She was never intimidated by her lack of money because, as she told Maxine, "You don't ever have to be ashamed of being poor if you know how to use soap and water, hammer and nails, and needle and thread."

1924–1930

Bricks

74" x 78"

Wool

Made by Mary Elizabeth Jennings Gledhill

(1887–1961)

Made in Vermilion, Sevier County, Utah

Owned by Maxine Roundy

Martha
Agnes
McKeachnie
Nielsen

■ ■

The Allotment Act of 1905 opened the Duchesne, Utah, area to homesteading. Under the act, Ute Indian land was taken from the reservation and given to the settlers. Among the first to stake a claim were Niels Eyner Nielsen and his father. Niels chose Indian Canyon for his ranch. He built a cabin, fenced the land, and brought in cattle, horses and sheep.

In 1911, Niels attended a dance in Vernal, Utah, where he noticed a beautiful girl in the crowd. He walked up to her and without asking her name said, "You're the prettiest girl here and someday I'm gonna marry you." The pretty girl, whose name was Agnes, replied, "And you're the craziest man here." They were married in 1912, and their first child was born nine months and three days later.

Agnes McKeachnie was born in Vernal in 1891 to a mother who had come from England and crossed the plains at age eleven with a handcart company. Agnes was a pretty girl, but slightly crippled in one foot, limping when she walked. A misguided principal suggested to her mother that she keep Agnes at home, so Agnes received a rather limited education. She became proficient at homemaking skills, which served her well when she married Niels and moved to his Duchesne ranch.

Although she married in the second decade of the twentieth century, Agnes's life in Duchesne was a frontier life. There was no electricity in her home until 1960 and no other conveniences such as a refrigerator or indoor plumbing. Meat was stored by hanging it in a tree during the night, then rolling it in a heavy quilt during the day to keep it cool. Dirty water was treated by putting a cut prickly pear in the water barrel. The floors were covered with homemade rag rugs, and all cooking was done on a woodburning stove. But Agnes was fussy and tidy and kept a clean house in spite of a lack of "modern conveniences" and a constant battle with the "dirty animals" she abhorred. From the spotless windows in the living room to the white George Washington spread that lay on her bed, Agnes's house was clean.

Agnes loved the Butterfly pattern. She stitched at least six of the quilts, one for each of her three daughters, two for granddaughters, and one for a niece. Her granddaughter Linda Olson received her quilt top for her wedding in 1960, made from fabrics her grandmother had pieced nearly thirty years earlier.

1930s

Butterflies

61″ x 83″

Cotton

Made by Martha Agnes McKeachnie
Nielsen (1891–1978)

Made in Duchesne, Duchesne County,
Utah

Owned by Linda Agnes Massey Olson

Sarah

Jennet

Carson

Lewis

Sarah Jennet Carson and Elizabeth Dennis were best friends. They shared secrets, walked together along Cherry Creek, and talked about their dreams and plans for the years to come. When Elizabeth married William Lewis, Sarah probably stitched on a quilt for her beloved friend. And when Elizabeth died at the young age of twenty-nine leaving four small sons, Sarah raised her best friend's children as her own after her marriage to William in 1890. Sarah and William eventually had six children of their own, five more sons and a daughter.

Sarah Carson's life began in Draper, Utah, on March 13, 1865. When she was eleven months old, her father moved the family to a one-room homesteading cabin in Richmond, a farming community in Cache County where the cattle and dairy business flourished. Indeed, Richmond boasted the first, and some would argue the best, creamery established in the area. The Carson family grew to include seven children. Sarah and her siblings were educated in the small schoolhouse in Richmond. She was a good student, but was especially proficient at sewing. At the age of eighteen she traveled to Salt Lake City to attend a dressmaking school and hone her homemaking skills. She married William Lewis when she was twenty-five.

Sarah and William raised a second family of young children when they were sixty years old. Their oldest son, Ralph, had lost his wife, leaving him with five children, ages two months to seven years. His wife's sister took the baby, and Grandma and Grandpa Lewis had the three older boys and one girl for six years until Ralph remarried. Alice, the little granddaughter, was given the Baby Blocks quilt top many years later

before Sarah died at the age of eighty-three in 1948.

Baby Blocks is a variation of the Tumbling Blocks pattern using large diamond shapes instead of the traditional small ones. Although the blocks appear to be square, they are actually constructed from three diamond-shaped pieces. The three-dimensional effect is created by piecing a medium-colored and a dark-colored diamond side to side and then using a light-colored piece at the top. The blocks then acquire their three dimensions no matter which way the quilt is turned. The piecing must be very carefully and methodically done so that the corners come together precisely to produce the desired geometric effect.

Sarah used scraps and flour sacks to piece her Baby Blocks quilt top. Some of the fabric may be as old as 1910 or 1915, but the piecing was not finished until the 1920s or 1930s. At least twenty-one of the pieces in the quilt were patched together to make a piece large enough to use, but Sarah did the piecing so carefully, it is difficult to detect. The top has never been washed and has been kept away from sunlight and moisture. The colors show no fading. Owner Janet Froh has decided never to quilt the top in order to preserve its historical integrity.

1920–1935

Baby Blocks

79" x 67"

Cotton

Made by Sarah Jennet Carson Lewis

(1865–1948)

Made in Richmond, Cache County, Utah

Owned by Janet Wayman Froh

Charlotte Swindlehurst spent a somewhat pampered childhood in Baxenden, Lancaster, England, for the first eleven years of her life. The family home had gas lights and water that was piped right into the kitchen. In 1868, the family sold many of their possessions and boarded the steamship *Colorado* to join the Mormons in Utah. Six hundred "Saints" composed the company, which arrived in New York City on July 28.

The company traveled by railroad as far as Brenton, Wyoming. Most of the younger passengers rode in cattle cars across the country; they had a wonderful time, shouting and bellowing like cows whenever a station was reached. The group reached Brenton on August 7, and prepared for the short journey through the mountains to Utah. The Swindlehurst family consisted of Charlotte, her parents, three sisters, and two brothers. Everyone able to walk was encouraged to do so. Charlotte later recalled that Fred Limb, who had come from Beaver, Utah, to assist in bringing the Saints westward, often let her and her younger sister Amelia ride in his wagon for a few miles when the road was good.

Beaver, two hundred miles south of Salt Lake City, became Charlotte's new home in September 1868. The family camped out the first night. In the morning, John Swindlehurst found better accommodations for his family in a small carpenter shop, where they stayed for three weeks. John quickly found work as a blacksmith, and soon they purchased a small home.

The Beaver Woolen Mill opened when Charlotte was fifteen years old. With her older sister Isabelle, who had learned to weave in England, she secured a job weaving cloth for men's suits. She was proud to tell her descendants she wove the cloth for the first suit of clothes her brother Joseph ever had.

Charlotte had been keeping company for a long time with a friendly, energetic young man named John Andrew Smith. In 1878, when they accompanied both sets of parents to St. George, Utah, John's father suggested that the couple get married right then to save a return trip in a few months. Charlotte and John protested at what they felt was a spontaneous and premature arrangement, but their arguments went unheard, and they were married on April 26 in the St. George L.D.S. Temple. They often joked with their children about the day they "had to get married."

Charlotte quit working at the woolen mill a year later. Her boss, John Ashworth, thanked her for six years of outstanding hard work with a gift of two blankets, a broom, and some milk pans, which the couple gratefully added to the meager housekeeping supplies in their new two-room house. It became their lifelong home and the birthplace of their eight children.

Through the Homestead Act John was able to secure a large section of land one mile north of town. To own the land, the family had to build a home on it and live there for six months each year for five years. Charlotte bravely met the challenge of the yearly moves to the little dirt-floored cabin, spending many of the long summer days with her young children in the coolness of the willow bower John had built. At the end of five years, the family celebrated having "proved up" on the land by adding two large rooms to the front of their home in Beaver. They never lived on the homestead farm again.

Charlotte was John's willing companion on many long excursions on horseback and by car. During one harrowing adventure, John overturned the car, and it slid thirty feet before coming to a stop. When the dust settled, it was discovered that the car had landed right side up with nothing more than a few scratches to the paint. Charlotte was surprised to find her glasses still in place. When the couples they were traveling with asked what he intended to do, John replied, "I intend to drive on." Charlotte and John celebrated sixty-two wedding anniversaries together before her death on September 5, 1940, at the age of eighty-three.

There are several names for the quilt pattern Charlotte Smith stitched in 1925—Double Monkey Wrench, Love Knot, Puss in the Corner, to mention a few, and Hole in the Barn Door, as the family refers to it. No one is certain what Charlotte called the design.

Charlotte
Swindlehurst
Smith

1925

Hole in the Barn Door

71" x 87"

Cotton

Made by Charlotte Swindlehurst Smith

(1857–1940)

Made in Beaver, Beaver County, Utah

Owned by Lavar Atkin

Article II of the bylaws of the national society of the Daughters of Utah Pioneers states that the association was created to review "the lives of the pioneers; thus teaching their descendants . . . lessons of faith, courage, fortitude, and patriotism." Nowhere are Utahns prouder of their pioneer heritage than in the D.U.P. camps of Brigham City and the small farming towns of Box Elder County.

The eastern and northern parts of Box Elder County were explored as early as the 1820s by fur trappers, such as Peter Skene Ogden and Joseph R. Walker, who traversed the area. Permanent settlements began in 1851, but the population mushroomed in 1853 when Lorenzo Snow was directed by Brigham Young to take fifty families to the Box Elder area and develop a cooperative community that could become self-sufficient. By the mid-1870s, the people of Brigham City were independent of the outside world, producing everything necessary to keep their large community running. Unfortunately, the co-op went into receivership in 1895, but it is still recognized as the first and most successful Mormon cooperative organization established by the Utah pioneers. Box Elder County also claims the distinction of joining the nation together on May 10, 1869, when the Central Pacific and the Union Pacific railroads met to complete the transcontinental line at Promontory Point. That event effectively put an end to the pioneer era.

In 1928 many of Box Elder County's pioneer descendants, members of the D.U.P. Locust Camp, organized a local fund-raiser. They would make a quilt, selling to camp members, their spouses, and their relatives the opportunity to have their names embroidered on it. A total of 795 people paid thirty cents each to have their names stitched either on one of the twenty-four wagon wheels running up and down the quilt or as part of the border that extends along three sides. Men's and women's names as well as two oxen-pulled covered wagons stitched in black decorate the unusual and intricate muslin top. The names are stitched in rose, blue, green, gold, and violet thread, and several of the wheels' centers are filled in with french knots.

The wagon wheels that spin across the surface of the quilt represent fourteen D.U.P. camps and company of the Box Elder region. The camps represented are Beehive, Deseret, Bear River, Fort Brigham, Garland, Honeysuckle, Locust, Midland, Oak, Perry, Sego Lily, Seagull, Sunflower, and Willow Creek. Quilting is done by hand with white thread around each of the twenty-four blocks, the outline of the embroidered wheels and the hub of each wheel.

The Friendship Wheel quilt of Box Elder County is presently stored at the Brigham City Museum. The south Box Elder County D.U.P. camps collectively own the quilt that displays the names of many "old-timers" who honored their pioneer ancestors with their contribution to the project.

1928–1930

Wheel Friendship Quilt

75½″ x 98″

Cotton

Made by Members of the Locust Camp of the Daughters of Utah Pioneers

Made in Brigham City, Box Elder County, Utah

Custodian: Brigham City Museum Gallery, South Box Elder County D.U.P.

Mary
Ellen
Bills
Seal

The couch in Ena Bodell's sewing room is piled with the whimsical pillows she makes whenever she samples a new quilt design. More samplers cover the walls and still more are neatly stored away in plastic boxes or in the closets that line one wall. On the opposite wall hangs the Log Cabin quilt made by Mary Ellen Seal, the grandmother of Ena's husband. It is a pale and subtle quilt, made in the coral and orange shades so popular during the 1930s, with touches of brown and blue and yellow. The hearth pieces of each block are a deep rust color quilted in coral thread, as are all the log cabin pieces, to match the cotton coral fabric used for the backing. There are twenty full blocks measuring seventeen inches each and one row of half blocks, perhaps to make the quilt fit a particular size bed.

Mary Ellen Bills began her life in South Jordan, Utah, in a little two-room house under a hill called Creek Bottom. She was the eighth of twelve children, born June 15, 1867, to William Andrew and Emeline Beckstead Bills. Mary learned responsibility and hard work at an early age. One of her chores was to carry drinking water from Beckstead Ditch to the house, an uphill climb. She was always careful not to spill, especially in the winter, when the water would freeze her fingers. She also gathered sagebrush and wood of any sort to keep the cooking fires going. Life in rural Utah was still a pioneering existence when Mary was growing up.

Mary fell in love with a young man who tended sheep for her father. Although Franklin Edward Seal was twenty-six years old and Mary had just turned fifteen, her parents consented to their marriage on August 10, 1882. They lived in South Jordan for two years, becoming the parents of a beautiful baby girl they named Lottie. In 1884, Franklin bought thirty-five acres of land to start his own farm. The ground was covered with sagebrush that needed to be cleared so the land could be cultivated and planted. Mary often put her baby in the shade behind a clump of bushes to protect her from the heat and helped her husband clear the ground.

Franklin built a one-room cabin for his family. Mary bore five children in that little dirt-floored shelter before a larger three-room home could be built just south of the original structure. A wooden floor was added in 1897. By 1899, Mary and Franklin had a family of seven children, which Mary was left to provide for when Franklin was called to serve a mission to England for the L.D.S. church. Four months after his departure, Mary gave birth to Mary Ellen. She took in washing, sewed rag rugs, and took care of new mothers and their babies for fifty cents a day. Sometimes her pay would be only a small amount of flour to make bread for her children. With hard work and careful managing, she was able to support her husband in the mission field and feed her family. After Franklin's return, four more children were added to the family, the twelfth being born in 1908.

Mary Ellen Seal was a masterful seamstress, making dozens of quilts. She was a charitable person too, neglecting her own concerns to help another in greater need. If there was work to be done, she was willing to lend an extra hand. She often helped her grown daughters bottle fruit, working faster than any of them and accomplishing more in a shorter time. She enjoyed community work projects, like cornhusking or fruit drying, when all the neighbors would gather at one house to work all day and then in the evening push back the scanty furniture and have a dance.

Her youngest daughter Bernice recalled that "Mother was always the happiest when she was keeping busy and helping someone."

When Franklin died in 1937, Mary must have recalled the tender poem he had written for her so long before. It reads in part:

I cannot bring you wealth, he said
I cannot bring you fame or place
Among the noted of the race
But I can love you.
When trials come to test you sweet
I can be sunlight to your feet
My kiss your precious lips shall
    greet
Because I love you.
I bow before no other shrine
If I go first across death's line
I will return to claim you mine
Because I love you.

Mary Ellen died fifteen years later, in 1952. She was eighty-four years old.

1930s

Log Cabin, Straight Furrows Setting

77" x 89"

Cotton

Made by Mary Ellen Bills Seal

(1867–1952)

Made in Riverton, Salt Lake County, Utah

Owned by Ena Bodell

Virginia
Saunders
Hunt

■ ■

A yo-yo is a child's toy, round and easily manipulated by attaching its string to one finger and spinning it up and down, up and down—a monotonous activity that can be performed by anyone with a yo-yo and a finger. In the hands of an expert, however, that spinning toy becomes a miracle of movement, twirling and twisting in maneuvers such as Around the World, Walking the Dog, Swinging in a Cradle. What appeared at first to be so easy and repetitive has now become an obvious expression of talent and persistence.

Making a fabric Yo-Yo is likewise a monotonous activity that can be performed by anyone with a fabric circle and a threaded needle. But here, too, in the hands of an expert, like Virginia Hunt, those redundant scrapbag circles become a flamboyant fabric display of six-pointed stars and tumbling, three-dimensional blocks—another obvious expression of talent and persistence.

Virginia Saunders Hunt was born at home in 1915, on land the family had owned in Salt Lake since building their first sod hut there in 1867. The youngest of seven children, she loved playing house, having tea parties, dressing up in her mother's long dresses, and sewing clothes for her dolls. Riding the ice wagon was a special treat, especially when she was given the reins. Her family and close friends called her "Sam," a name given her by an older brother when she was born.

Virginia graduated from East High School in 1933 and attended the University of Utah for a year before transferring to L.D.S. Business College. When she was twenty-one, she served a mission in Canada. When she was thirty-five and employed by the Internal Revenue Service in Washington, D.C., she met Eldon Hunt. When she and Eldon married in the Salt Lake L.D.S.

Temple, she wore the wedding dress her mother had worn in 1899. A daughter and a son were born into the Hunt family.

Virginia's daughter, Marsha, remembers her mother as "a five-foot-two-inch bundle of energy." She was like a magnet, pulling the family together for wonderful parties and dinners. She gardened and cooked with the same level of energy she applied to everything else. She could knit, do needlepoint, embroider, and crochet. She also made quilts, but she did not leave many of them behind, preferring to give most of them away. Virginia belonged to a quilt club and met regularly with her like-minded friends. An avid reader, she often quoted from Stevenson's *A Child's Garden of Verse*, especially "My Shadow."

When her children entered middle school, Virginia went to work as a secretary at East High School. Upon retirement, she and Eldon served an L.D.S. mission to Vienna, Austria. For many years, she cared untiringly for her aging mother, her mother-in-law, and her sister. Marsha, who now owns the Yo-Yo quilt, remembers her mother as "ever young," a woman who sincerely enjoyed her ten grandchildren, her friends, her needlework, and serving others. Virginia died in an automobile accident while traveling with Eldon in Europe in 1992.

1930s

Yo-Yo Quilt

85″ x 101″

Cotton

Made by Virginia Saunders Hunt

(1915–1992)

Made in Salt Lake City, Salt Lake County,
Utah

Owned by Marsha Hunt Buccambuso

Edith

Ione

Cato

Johnston

Edith Johnston is a true original, enamored of life and eager to learn everything she can about anything that interests her. She is a rock hound, which led her to become an expert silversmith, skilled at fashioning elaborate settings for the stones, dinosaur bones, and pieces of petrified wood she and her husband have collected. She is a historian, knowledgeable about the old mining towns that have provided her with the more than 800 antique bottles she displays in her living room and the thousands more in storage. She has a talent for knowing exactly where to dig for the fossils she admires. And she is an expert seamstress who sewed buckskin jackets on the hand-turned New National sewing machine she inherited sixty years ago from an aunt who had gotten it years before that from a very old lady. She is curious, hard working, creative, and only eighty-five years old.

Edith is a native Utahn, although she was born in 1911 in Grand Junction, Colorado, because that was the city closest to her home in Cisco, Utah. She married Wayne Johnston in 1929, and the two lived in Cisco until moving to Price in 1938. Wayne was a livestock auctioneer and a cattleman. Edith worked at his side, driving the big cattle trucks with ease. "I cried when we had to sell those trucks," she remembers, thinking about Wayne's retirement.

Early in her marriage, Edith decided to commemorate the family business by stitching the Johnston cattle brands into a unique quilt. The family used two brands to identify its cattle: the Swastika, a symbol that originated in Greece, and the X-Diamond-X. She pieced the Swastikas from sewing scraps and her collection of Bull Durham tobacco sacks, small muslin bags measuring approximately three inches by two inches, stitched on two sides and the bottom, with a cord in a casing at the top. Children often used the empty bags to hold marbles or tiny keepsakes and trinkets. Edith gathered and picked apart 110 of the little sacks to make her quilt blocks.

She finished the machine piecing of the quilt top in 1933, but was unable to quilt it at that time. The family lived in a one-room log cabin, and there was no space to set up a quilt. It wasn't until thirty years later that she added a back and batting to the quilt. She stitched around each Swastika with pale pink thread and on the plain blocks she quilted the X-Diamond-X brand. The quilt backing was brought to the front and machine stitched in pink thread.

Edith and Wayne raised four children in Price, two girls and two boys. At last count they have twenty-four great-grandchildren. In 1994, they celebrated their sixty-fourth wedding anniversary.

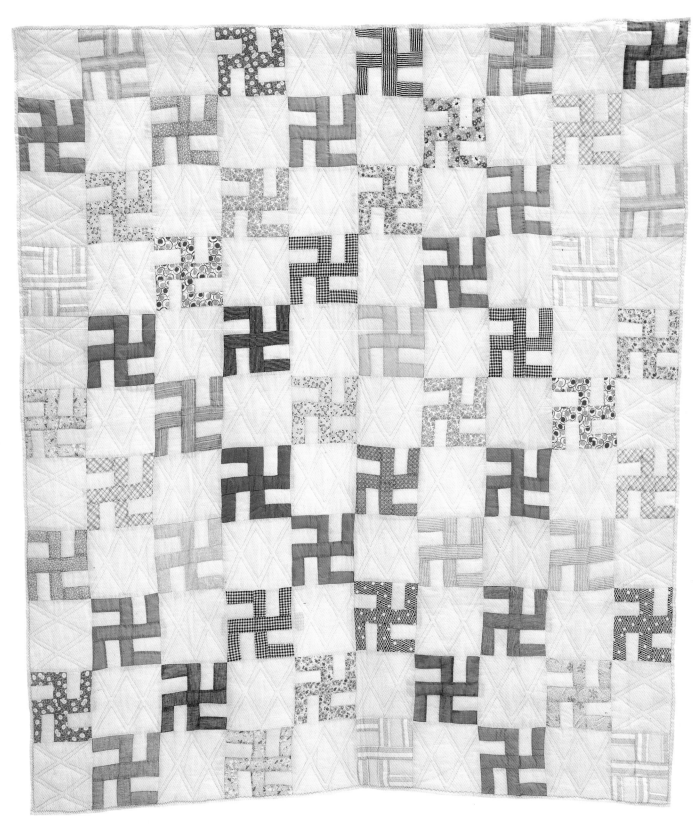

1933

Cattle Brand

74″ x 83″

Cotton

Made by Edith Ione Cato Johnston

(1911–)

Made in Cisco, Grand County, Utah

Owned by the maker

Annie White Johnson

Mary Ann Pratt was two years old when her mother, Sarah, died in 1878. Joseph Pratt was left with the overwhelming task of caring for five young sons and two daughters. When Mary Ann was three years old, a childless friend of her mother's offered to adopt the sickly little girl and raise her as her own child. Joseph did not want to separate the family, but there seemed no other solution. Mary Ann was legally adopted by Diana and Barnard White and known for the rest of her life as "Annie."

When Annie was seven years old, Father White bought a farm in Perry, Utah, then known as Three Mile Creek because of its distance from Brigham City. Annie and her mother moved to the farm six months later to make their home. Life went on peacefully until January 1886, when Diana passed away after a three-week battle with typhoid fever. Ten-year-old Annie became part of her father's second family when his other wife, Jane, and her children moved onto the farm.

These were the days of polygamy raids against the Mormons, and the White family was deeply involved in the Mormon "underground." Many nights Annie would fall asleep with her own family, only to discover the next morning that two or three other families had come in the night. She never knew their real names, but was told to address them as Mrs. Davis, Mrs. Taylor, Mr. Smith. One of her favorite visitors was Joseph Fielding Smith, who became president of the L.D.S. church in 1901. He called Annie's home "Camp Serene" and stayed there for weeks at a time. He was on the run from federal authorities from 1883 to 1887. Whenever he was a guest, it was Annie's job during mealtime to watch from the upstairs windows for U.S. marshals. When her warning cries came, the dining room was quickly cleared and the fugitives safely hidden away. It was usually a false alarm, but Smith told Annie he never worried about being taken when she was on guard. After the Woodruff Manifesto prohibiting plural marriages was passed in 1890, company at the White home decreased significantly.

Although Annie's family was geographically isolated, her father's business travels brought the family in contact with many modern, labor-saving devices. Once he brought home a mangle to help with the ironing. It consisted of two wooden rollers on an iron frame that was turned with a handle. It was still very physical work, but ironing flat items was much easier, as long as they were folded, smoothed, and put through the device several times. Ruffles, tucks, and frills still had to be ironed by hand, which meant fires to heat the irons, even on the hottest summer days.

Annie married Oluf Johnson in the Salt Lake L.D.S. Temple in 1902. They spent their first year as a married couple in the home of Oluf's mother in Brigham City, Utah. In the spring of 1903, Oluf went to Garland, Utah, to put in crops on his land and build a two-room house. He was called back home suddenly when Annie became extremely ill before the birth of their first child. The baby boy was stillborn. Eclampsia caused Annie to go into convulsions, and she remained unconscious for five days. Slowly she recovered, moving to her new home in Garland two months later. During the course of the next seventeen years, she gave birth to seven more children. Of the four boys and four girls she bore, only three daughters survived, but she was grateful, as she wrote in her autobiography: "We were always thankful we had that many, as the doctors said we would never have any that would live."

Annie eventually had thirteen grandchildren, and she made an appliqued quilt top for each one of them. The Morning Glory quilt was made from a kit in 1935 for granddaughter Mary Ann Creer. It has many excellent characteristics, not the least of which is the unusual blue border with the inside scallop. The quilted bows between the embroidered groups of morning glories add whimsical charm to the beautiful bedcover.

1935

Morning Glory

74¼" x 92"

Cotton

Made by Annie White Johnson

(1876–1965)

Made in Garland, Box Elder County, Utah

Owned by Mary Ann Creer

Emma Sophia Elizabeth Morrell used scraps from the dresses of her daughters to piece this Sunflower quilt for her youngest daughter, Dimple, in 1935. Up to that time, she had made heavy, practical camp quilts, but now she ventured into quilt making that was more pleasing to the soul, though still as useful. The unusual yellow-centered flowers on one of her first attempts are beautifully hand appliqued with a blanket stitch in black. They peek from the spaces of the loosely woven blue and white striped sashing that sets the blocks together. The top is hand quilted with blue thread.

Emma was born in 1871 to George and Maria Albrecht of Wismar, Germany. She started school at age six, going every day except Sunday and Christmas. She learned to knit and sew the first year. The Bible was the text-book from which she was required to learn three verses a day. "If you didn't know your verses," she said, "you were given a licking." School was an expensive privilege not to be carelessly dismissed. If a child was absent and neglected to bring a written excuse, "It would cost your parents as much as it would to send you to school a whole year."

Emma continued her German schooling for two years, walking the half mile to school and home each day, as well as at lunchtime. The family was not wealthy, but they lived comfortably. Meals consisted of rye bread, butter, milk, dried fruits, and meat once a day. At Christmastime a biscuit with a raisin in the top was a special treat.

On October 1, 1880, when Emma was eight years old, the family left Wismar for America and Utah. In what seemed a blur of boats and trains, Emma recalled that they went by train to Hamburg, then sailed for two days as they crossed the North Sea to Liverpool, England. Another train ride across England took them to the steamship *Wisconsin*, which they boarded to cross the Atlantic Ocean. Eleven days later they were in New York City, where they rode a train west to Salt Lake City. After six days in the city, they traveled to Manti, Utah, where Emma's father, George Albrecht, began working on the Manti L.D.S. Temple.

Emma returned to school during her first winter in Manti, but the family soon moved to the small town of Dover, Utah. Emma started hiring out, working at age eleven for a man named Jim Hill. For six weeks of labor, she earned a pair of shoes, a slip, and an apron. When she was twelve, Emma's baby brother, Jacob, was born. She was needed at home, where she took on all the household chores for her ailing mother.

In 1888, when she was nearly seventeen years old, Emma married George Morrell, originally from Kamas, Utah. They settled in Fremont, Utah, where she bore fourteen children. A son and daughter died at the age of two months, but the remaining twelve children grew to adulthood. Dimple is the youngest and the only surviving child of Emma and George. Emma died in 1950 at the age of seventy-nine.

Emma
Albrecht
Morrell

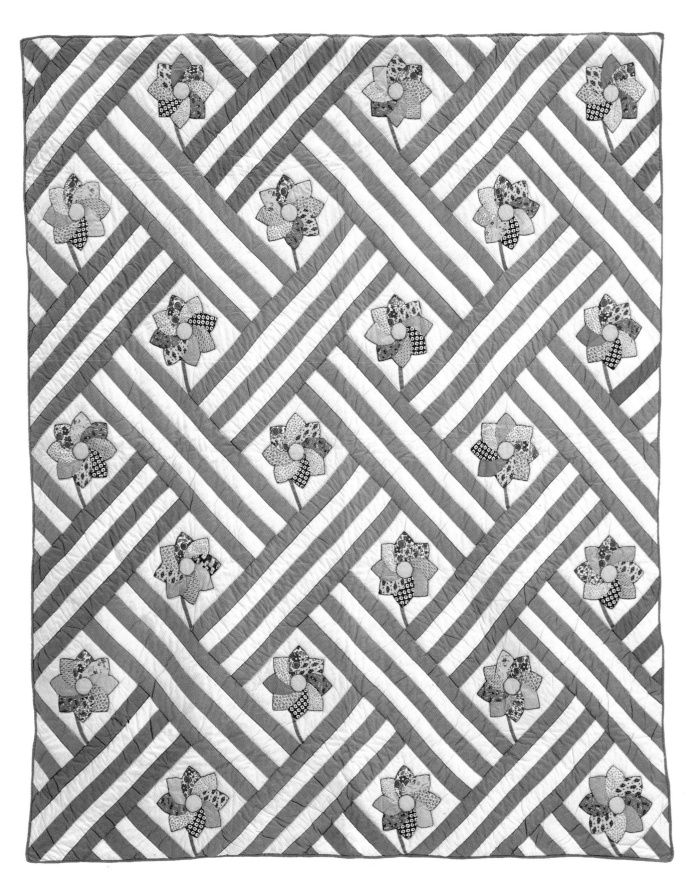

1935

Sunflower

76" x 94"

Cotton

Made by Emma Albrecht Morrell

(1871–1950)

Made in Fremont, Wayne County, Utah

Owned by Dimple Morrell Flugrad

Ella Hammond Campbell

The Providence Block was a popular pattern in the little town of Providence, Utah, during the 1930s and 1940s. Ella Campbell made at least three quilts using the distinctive design. Quilt owner Barbara Campbell recalls that anyone who enjoyed quilting during that era made at least one quilt using the pattern. Her husband's grandmother referred to it as The Fallen Leaf. The design of the block is like Bay Leaf; the quilters of the northern Utah area added an additional "leaf" reaching diagonally into each corner, and claim the composition as their own.

Ella set her twenty appliqued and embroidered blocks into a beautiful pale peach sashing that highlights the wonderful assortment of scrapbag prints she had assembled over the years. Although each petal-shaped piece appears at first glance to be of a different fabric, upon closer observation a careful and symmetrical arrangement is obvious. For example, each corner piece is made of the same fabric as the piece that is diagonally across from it, and the skillful distribution of dark and light fabrics balances the variety of prints and colors in the quilt.

Clyde Campbell's grandmother gave this quilt to him when he graduated from high school. He has vivid memories of quilting days at his home, with his mother and grandmother in a room filled with women stitching and chatting. He always ate well on those occasions.

Ella Hammond was born April 16, 1865, in the six-year-old settlement of Providence, Utah. She was the oldest of ten children born to Milton Datus and Freelove Miller Hammond. In a short autobiography written in 1832, she recalled her family's pioneering experiences:

> Mother had a loom in our living room, she wove cloth and carpet. I remember wearing shoes the upper part being made from pieces of father's worn-out suits. The shoemaker put soles and heels on them. We did not actually suffer for food but we sometimes had a rather scant living, when we had mush and milk for supper. . . . No cream or sugar either.

Ella attended school in Providence until she was fourteen years old, when her mother died just one week after giving birth to her tenth child. Two baby girls had died earlier, leaving Milton with eight young children. He had to make a living for the family, so six of the children were sent to Aunt Lovisa's and the other two lived with Aunt Chesty. Ella writes, "They were noble women and very kind to us. I have thought so much about it since I have grown older, what it meant to them to have so many children added to their already large families. They made good homes for us."

Shortly after her mother's death, Ella traveled to Montana with her father who had contracted to do rock work in Beaver Canyon. The girl who had been cooking for the eighteen men in camp developed an infection in her hand, and Ella was persuaded to take over her job. For four weeks she cooked for the friendly, hungry men, whom she knew from Providence. She never forgot their generous praise and encouragement to her during this difficult time in her life.

When she returned to school in the fall, she began having trouble seeing. She was so sensitive about her problem that she quit school and would not tell her father why. He offered to send her to Salt Lake or Provo, but Ella refused. At that time, none of the young people Ella knew wore glasses, and she never even considered it to be an option.

Ella worked in her brother's bookstore in Logan for several years before marrying Joseph Campbell in September 1887. Their first daughter, Irene, was born in July 1888, and Vesta followed in April 1891, just a few weeks before Joseph was to leave to serve a two-year mission in England. He left in October instead, returning in the fall of 1893. Between 1894 and 1905, six more children were born to Ella and Joseph, including twin daughters born in 1901. Ella was left at home once again in 1907—this time with eight children— when Joseph was called to another mission in the northern states. "It was quite a struggle for us," she writes, "for there were eight children, our oldest boy was only nine years old, but with hard work we managed to get along."

Although Ella experienced great sorrow, labor, and hardship during her life, she considered herself to be greatly blessed, especially where her children were concerned. In 1932, she wrote that she and Joseph had thirty-two living grandchildren and three great-grandchildren. The numbers have no doubt increased dramatically since then, and so have the blessings.

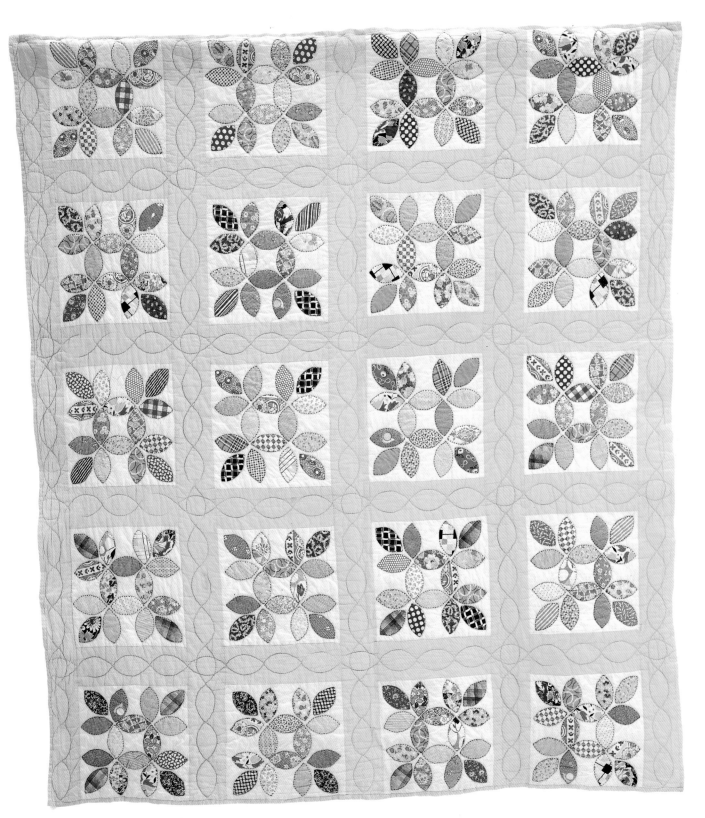

1935

The Fallen Leaf:
Providence Block

67" x 78"

Cotton

Made by Ella Hammond Campbell

(1865–1945)

Made in Providence, Cache County, Utah

Owned by Barbara D. Campbell

Mary
Roskelley

The Roskelley clan was a family that worked together, sons and daughters alike. Homesteading was a difficult life, and everyone pitched in milking cows, raising pigs and chickens, and tending to the crops. In the Roskelley family hard work and cooperation were especially important because father Samuel Roskelley had four living wives and not enough time to spend with each of them in taking care of the farming and the chores. Of necessity, a polygamous wife and her children spent much of their time working and surviving on their own.

Mary Roberts was one of five wives taken by Samuel Roskelley, and the mother of two sons and five daughters. She also raised four sons left motherless when Samuel's first wife died, as well as becoming mother to an unrelated baby girl whose own mother had died shortly after her birth. It was Mary's daughter and namesake, Mary Roskelley, who made this elegant wool quilt. Known as May, she was the third child born to Mary and Samuel. Being one of the oldest in the family, she spent many hours helping her mother care for the younger children and work the farm.

May Roskelley was born in Smithfield, Utah, on March 10, 1870. She was an educated woman for her time, progressing through public school and attending one year at the Brigham Young College in Logan. For financial reasons, she was forced to discontinue her schooling and hire out as a domestic to help make a living for her family. Although she was unable to graduate from college and receive a degree, she was well known for her nursing skills and was often called upon to perform medical duties.

During antipolygamy raids in Cache County in 1888, May became her father's escort when Samuel had to go to Logan to hide from federal authorities. May would often ride the six-mile distance on horseback to bring him home when the danger had passed or to take him back to Logan to hide if necessary. In January 1889, he was arrested for having more wives than the law allowed, but charges were eventually dropped. At the time, he had four wives and twenty-two children.

When she was in her twenties, May left home and spent most of the next nine years as a cook at a sawmill in Gentile Valley, Idaho. After returning home, she began working at the Cache Knitting Factory in Logan as a cutter and finisher; she worked there until retiring. She salvaged wool scraps from the cutting floor of the factory, using them for her beautiful quilt tops. She often pieced the tops with the help of her sister Cassie and quilted them with Cassie and their youngest sister, Druzilla. This is probably the team that made the Lattice quilt which was given to May's niece Arnona in 1935. May made quilts for each of her nieces and nephews, of which there were many. She died at the age of seventy-two. She had never married.

The allure of this quilt is perceived through touch. The colors and design may be subtle and conservative, but this is a very exciting, tactile quilt, soft and sensuous. To touch it is to love it and to become enchanted with the interesting qualities of wool. Finely woven wool can be pliable, smooth, and almost silky. It can be beautiful, like May Roskelley's quilt.

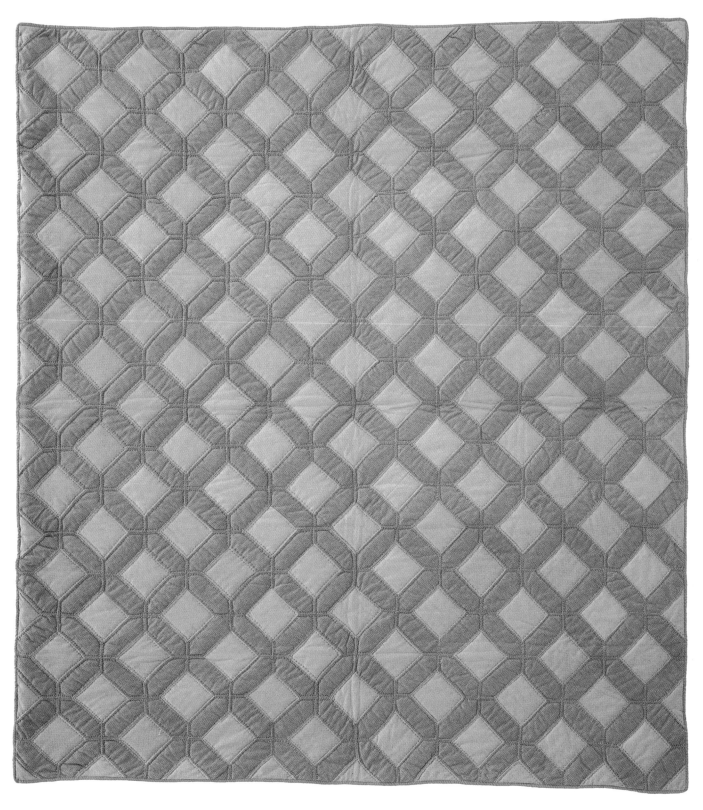

1935

Lattice

81″ x 93″

Wool and Cotton

Made by Mary Roskelley (1870–1942)

Made in Smithfield, Cache County, Utah

Owned by Arnona Blanchard Dattage

Benjamin Franklin so admired the wild turkeys of North America that he suggested they be chosen as the national emblem of the United States. He saw them as proud, swift, clever birds that seemed the perfect symbol for an independent young nation in the new world. But Mr. Franklin was looking at wild specimens, and had never spent a summer herding the domesticated variety or "the stupid, recalcitrant fowls," as Donna Harward describes them. If he had, he might have changed his mind.

Donna Harward will never forget the summer of 1936 in the little Utah town of Aurora. While her husband worked for a dollar a day on the Scorup Ranch, she shepherded a flock of pesky baby turkeys. Each morning she hiked several miles out of town, crossing the Sevier River to save time, with her lunch under one arm and her year-old daughter, Carol, under the other. She passed the slow days chasing unruly birds out of grainfields and tending her baby inside a hot, dusty tent.

Donna's sister gave her a piece of blue and white gingham fabric, and she began cutting quilt blocks to ease the monotonous routine. The white pieces in the quilt came from used, cotton clay bags given to Donna by her mother-in-law, Sarah Jeanette Harward. The clay mill in Aurora gave local residents the torn or imperfect bags to use for home sewing. Sarah made sheets, pillowcases, dish towels, petticoats, and even white pajamas for her husband from the cast-off bags. Now Donna used them for her turkey quilt squares, carrying the fabric and a pair of scissors in a paper sack every day, hiking her skirts up to cross the river with her baby.

In the evenings while her husband took the night shift with the turkeys, Donna machine stitched her blue and white squares together. She washed the clay bags on a washboard and dyed them blue, then pieced them together for the backing. When the quilt top was completed, it was too plain for Donna. She appliqued small blue triangles into the corners where the white points meet, giving the quilt a feeling of movement like a field of spinning pinwheels. The original design of the border echoes that feeling with its train track or highway motif.

The batting inside the quilt came from the sheep of Grass Valley Ranch, owned by Donna's father, near Koosharem, Utah. The hand-clipped wool, dirty with natural lanolin, sand, and burrs, was gently washed in tubs of warm water and spread outside in the sun to dry. The resulting hard knots of wool were tediously carded by hand, slowly softened into fluffy little batts. The batts were then laid row by row onto the quilt backing which had been stretched and tacked onto wooden frames, and the quilt top was added and quilted to outline the pieced shapes.

During the years of constant use, the quilt was protected from dirty hands and faces by a "quilt petticoat" made of flour sacks. The petticoat was basted onto one end of the quilt, extending eighteen inches beyond the quilt edge. The petticoat was washed instead of the quilt, sparing it from unneeded laundering which would have eventually shrunk and flattened the wool batts.

As she looks at the quilt after sixty years, Donna recalls the smell of turkeys and the wet, early-morning treks across the Sevier River. She also remembers tender moments with her baby daughter and reflects that "sometimes the seeming hardships of yesteryear are the sweet memories of today."

If the blue and white quilt of Donna's turkey days was too plain, the quilt top she received as a wedding gift in 1934 was just too busy. She carefully removed some of the plaid blocks before quilting it and replaced them with plain blue chambray. With her reputation for "making things over" it came as a surprise to no one.

The pieces in the quilt are scraps from Donna's older brother's home-made shirts and the aprons her mother always wore. There is a question as to who pieced the quilt, since it was made either before Donna was born or when she was a small child. The two possible seamstresses are Elizabeth Wright— Aunt Lizzie—and Regina Mortensen— Aunt Geenie. Both women did sewing for Donna's mother in return for fresh milk, butter, lard, sausage, soup bones, and home-baked bread.

Aunt Lizzie was the spinster sister of an uncle and lived in a little house with a combination bedroom/living room. The walls were covered with newspapers. Donna remembers her rocking and knitting, rocking and knitting, her needles keeping rhythm with the squeak of the old rocking chair.

Aunt Geenie was the wife of Great-uncle John, Grandfather Mortenson's brother. The childless couple had come from Norway, and lived in a log cabin across the street from Donna. Aunt Geenie was a professional dressmaker. Her young niece often watched her lay fabrics on her high bed and cut out dresses and shirts without a pattern. Donna possesses the same knack and has never used a pattern on any of the quilts she has constructed. Nor has she ever purchased fabric to make her quilts. She only uses scraps because "that's where quilts come from."

1936

Blue and White Checks

74" x 80"

Cotton

Made and owned by Donna B.
Harward (1913–)
Made in Aurora, Sevier
County, Utah

Donna
Harward

Before 1918

Jacob's Ladder

66" x 77"

Cotton

Made by Elizabeth Wright or
Regina Mortensen
Made in Koosharem, Sevier
County, Utah
Owned by Donna B. Harward

Veda
Behunin

The patchwork quilt was born of necessity and economy. Colonial and frontier seamstresses used the precious, costly cotton and woolen scraps left over from household sewing projects to stitch something warm and useful. Material from seams and unworn places in discarded clothing could be cut into squares, diamonds, and triangles and pieced into an Irish Chain, Blazing Star, or Tree of Life quilt top. Even though many elaborate, sophisticated designs arose from the humble pieced quilt, appliqued quilts were for many years thought to be superior to and more elegant than their primitive cousins.

The Broken Star is a complicated pattern that rivals any appliqued design. It can be very difficult to piece and sew correctly because of its tendency to buckle if the pieces are not perfectly matched. Collectors know that it is not uncommon to find an unfinished Broken Star quilt concealed in an attic trunk, hidden away by a maker who was too frustrated to undo and restitch the pieces, but too frugal to discard them. Veda Behunin of Boulder, Utah, expertly pieced a Broken Star quilt top in the 1930s that surpasses many quilts, both appliqued and pieced, in its outstanding design and execution. It will never be found hidden in an attic trunk.

There are several remarkable things about Veda's Broken Star quilt, not the least of which is that she does not remember making it. Her sister-in-law Faye Behunin remembers receiving the top as a wedding gift in 1940; she added the outside blue squares so that it would look "like a star in the sky" and quilted it six or eight years later. But Veda, who is a prolific quilter and continues to quilt, has no recollection of the masterpiece she created sixty years ago. She recently finished another Broken Star quilt that covers her bed in Boulder.

The Broken Star pattern was designed to evoke the image of an exploding star, and the Behunin quilt pulsates with an astounding vibrancy that could easily preface such a cosmic event. Each diamond is formed from thirty-six smaller diamonds that range in color from rust to orange to peach to pale yellow to off-white and back again. Both the deliberate choice of rust-colored diamonds and their placement in the design especially intensify the sense of explosion after explosion in a bright night sky.

Eight large diamonds form the central star and focal point of the quilt. Each of the eight outer points bursts into three more diamonds that fuse into a total of twenty-four diamonds bordering the design. The eight-pointed star has become a sixteen-pointed star flying outward into the heavens. It is indeed remarkable that such a complex effect can be achieved by the simple repetition of fabric pieces of the same size and shape. Quilting on the diamonds is done "in the ditch" (stitches quilted close to the seam rather than a quarter inch away). The blue, set-in blocks are quilted in a spider web pattern using blue thread.

1930–1940

Broken Star

74" x 74"

Cotton

Pieced by Veda Behunin

Quilted by Faye Behunin

Made in Boulder, Garfield County, Utah,

and in Torrey, Wayne County, Utah

Owned by Faye Behunin

Inez
Heaton
Hoyt

Jeana Jones Kimball is a well-known Utah quilter, designer, author, and lecturer. The small quilt hanging on her living room wall—a delightful gathering of brown bunnies hopping through twisting, green vines cut from vintage 1930s fabric and appliqued on a white background—is ample evidence of her quilting and designing skills. She grew up in a world where her grandmother always had a quilt "on" and her grandfather drew pattern templates for his wife's creations. Jeana learned to use a sewing machine by piecing quilts. One of her sweetest memories is the day she went to her Grandma Hoyt's home, shortly before leaving for college in Salt Lake City, and laid out some squares she had pieced as a girl. Together, they decided on the best design layout, cutting fabric from an old, full-skirted dress for the sashing. As they worked, Jeana listened to her grandmother talk about her life and the world when she was a teenager.

Inez Heaton was born and raised in the tiny southern Utah town of Orderville at the end of the nineteenth century. Orderville has a unique history dating back to 1875, when the community was established at the request of Brigham Young, president of the L.D.S. church. The families called to settle there were to live the "United Order of Enoch," a voluntary, communal, self-sufficient way of life. Inez Heaton's grandfather William and his family were part of the original group of settlers in 1869.

Of the more than 200 "orders" established in Utah, southern Idaho, northern Arizona, and Nevada, Orderville, Utah, was the most famous

example. The members of these United Orders contributed all their property and labor to a common pool from which each person drew to satisfy physical needs. Because President Young left the day-to-day operation of the orders in the hands of the local leaders, several different interpretations of the United Order emerged. Orderville discontinued the practice of the United Order in 1885, just six years before Inez was born there.

The Bow Tie quilt Inez made in the 1930s was one of her favorite patterns. Her daughter, Loraine Hoyt Jones, recalls her mother making several of them, although this is the only one remaining. The colors and prints in the quilt provide a wonderful sampling of the fabrics of that era, especially the Nile green fabric, which Jeana calls "that green," which was so commonly used during the Great Depression. The quilt has a thick cotton batt, and the edges are unusually thick; it appears that Inez folded the backing twice before stitching it along the front edge of the quilt.

Inez married Frederick Cross Hoyt in 1912, and they raised eight children, six boys and two girls. Most of the scraps cut and pieced in the Bow Tie quilt came from the sewing she did for her children. Fred was the postmaster of Orderville as well as a farmer. When he had animals to tend to in the afternoon, Inez would wash up, put on a clean apron, and head over to the post office to finish up for him. Fred enjoyed helping Inez with her patterns, and would even thread needles for her when he had time.

In 1960, Inez and Fred moved to St. George, Utah, less than a hundred miles from Orderville. Here she spent the final seventeen years of her life, enjoying her grandchildren. Jeana especially

remembers her love of music and the piano in her house. When one of the grandchildren would plink on the keys, she would hum whatever tune it reminded her of, changing the tune as the child found new keys to pound on. Inez died at the age of eighty-six.

1930–1940

Bow Tie

62″ x 68″

Cotton

Made by Inez Heaton Hoyt (1891–1977)

Made in Orderville, Kane County, Utah

Owned by Jeana Jones Kimball

Quilting is one of the oldest forms of needlework, dating back to the eleventh century in Europe. Although it may have originated as a method for increasing the warmth of fabrics, it soon became much more than stitching two pieces of material together with padding in the middle. Elaborate designs began to emerge on personal articles of clothing such as petticoats and on special creations like wedding quilts. The artistry and stature of a quilter could be measured by the number of tiny, even stitches on her quilted surfaces. The Whole Cloth quilt became an especially effective medium for displaying such proficiency, even after the revival of patchwork quilting in the twentieth century. The gold Whole Cloth quilt sewn by a group of quilters in Wellsville in 1938 is an outstanding example of the art form.

Wellsville, Utah, was originally settled in 1856 by twenty-five people from the families of Peter, John, and William Maughan, Zial Riggs, and Francis W. Gunnell, as well as two single men, George Bryan and O. D. Thompson. The town was known as Maughan's Fort until 1859, when it was renamed Wellsville in honor of Daniel Wells, a counselor to President Brigham Young. In 1863, the town was surveyed and laid out as a typical Mormon community oriented to the four points of the compass with all streets meeting at right angles. Land was divided into ten-acre blocks, with each block sectioned into eight 1.25-acre lots. The city was incorporated in 1866.

Quilting bees probably began in Wellsville as soon as the first women had settled into their temporary wagon-box homes. The quilting bee delivered many pioneer women from the isolation their lifestyle dictated. More formalized "quilting clubs" came later, when an increase in population made socializing easier and less of an issue. Quilters became a more elite and specialized group of women whose main interest in meeting together was to quilt and whose primary interest in quilting was beauty rather than necessity.

In Wellsville, organized quilting was an integral part of each L.D.S. ward's Relief Society. Members of each group met regularly at their neighborhood wardhouse to trace, cut, piece, and quilt for new babies and new brides in the area. Once a year the Relief Societies of all the wards combined their talents to create a quilt to be donated to the annual town Founder's Day celebration held on Labor Day. The quilt was usually a Whole Cloth design showcasing the members' stitching virtuosity. During the month of August, the coveted prize hung in the window of the local lumber store, where chances to win it were sold until Founder's Day.

In 1938, Ray P. Hill bought a chance on the golden quilt. Just before the raffle began, Ellen Jones, who was engaged to marry his son, Ray M., mentioned that she really would like to have that quilt. In jest, Ray P. said if he won the quilt, he would give it to her as a wedding present. Ray P. did win the quilt, and true to his word, he presented it to Ellen, much to the dismay of his wife who had probably worked on the quilt with her Relief Society group and wanted it for herself.

There was a small faded area in one corner of the quilt, the result of its month-long display in the window of the lumber store, but Ellen was pleased with the precise stitching on the center medallion, the crosshatch quilting, and the scalloped border. There are eight tiny, even stitches to the inch. Hearts and flowers are also stitched into the smooth satin surface. Lucinda Hill now owns her mother's treasured Founder's Day wedding quilt.

1937

Satin Whole Cloth Quilt

82″ x 86″

Satin

Made by the combined Relief Societies of
the Wellsville L.D.S. Wards

Made in Wellsville, Cache County, Utah

Owned by Lucinda Hill

Elizabeth
Luella
Williams
Thompson

■ ■

The incredible variety of fabrics in Luella Thompson's Nosegay quilt makes it a truly fascinating example of Depression era craftsmanship. It would be difficult to find many of the prints repeated in the 560 machine-pieced fabric shapes she chose to create her floral fanfare. According to her granddaughter Helen Lee, the peach sashing was one of Luella's favorite colors, along with green and purple, and she incorporated it into her quilt patterns whenever possible. She used a treadle machine to piece the blocks. It was not unusual for her to have a quilt on the frame for friends or neighbors to stitch on when they came visiting. If they could stay all day, she thanked them with a delicious meal.

Perhaps the quilting on the Nosegay quilt was done during one of Luella's impromptu quilting bees. It is just as beautiful as the piecing. Each of the six pieces that make up the bouquet is quilted around the outside edge, with several rows of stitching fanning out across the entire nosegay. The handles have a petal shape quilted in with the same shape repeated in the spaces between the handles. The peach sashing is done in a cable motif with the petal shape repeated throughout.

Her granddaughter Helen Lee says that Luella loved to quilt, and "was always generous in giving away the things she had made, including her quilts." She made quilts for each of her five children, her nine grandchildren, and most of her twenty-eight great-grandchildren before she passed away in 1966. The Nosegay quilt was originally a gift to her oldest son, Warren, and his wife, Pearl. In addition to her quilting, Luella also enjoyed doing other types of handwork, especially embroidery and crocheting.

Luella was born in Beaver, Utah, in 1879 to Nephi and Martha Moyes Williams, one of four daughters. She married James Alva Thompson in 1901. They made their home in Beaver, where they reared three sons and two daughters; another son had died as an infant. Helen Lee describes her grandmother Luella as a person with "a pleasant disposition, a kind smile, and was a pleasure to be around."

1937

Nosegay

72" x 84"

Cotton

Made by Elizabeth Luella Williams
Thompson (1879–1966)

Made in Beaver, Beaver County, Utah

Owned by George Reed Thompson

Evelyn Nebeker once made thirty quilts in six years. Not bad, considering she had never even seen a quilt until she got married. Her mother-in-law, Minerva Nebeker, had asked her if she could use a thimble, and Evelyn's affirmative reply led to a lifelong love of quilt making. Even her husband, Ned, became involved in the venture, taking an occasional stitch on a quilt when he thought no one was looking. The batting Evelyn used in her quilts was made with Ned's help. His unusual wool-gathering method was to kill the sheep, put the meat in the meat house, hang the pelt over the fence to dry, cut the pelt into strips, wash the strips, shear the wool off the pelts, and card the wool into small batts, which Evelyn then laid out on the quilt backing.

Evelyn's parents, Arnison and Amelia Wilson Hoskisson, had come to Salt Lake by way of Yorkshire, England. Arnison made a handsome living for his family of nine children with the sixteen grocery stores he owned. Evelyn loved to bag groceries in the store before her father sold his stores to a large chain.

In 1933, when she was twenty-five, Evelyn married her best friend's cousin, Ned Bingham Nebeker from Payson, Utah. Ned and Evelyn settled in Daggett County on the Connor Basin Ranch, which belonged to Ned's family. For fifteen years they worked the ranch and raised their two children. At first, they lived in the "long house" with Ned's mother and his aunt and uncle and their son and daughter-in-law. The house was built with a living room in the center, a kitchen on each end of the living room, and bedrooms strung out behind the kitchens. Soon Ned built Evelyn a new log house with a large living room, one kitchen, two bedrooms, and a big, rock fireplace Evelyn loved.

When time allowed, Evelyn quilted. She sewed thirty quilts between 1933 and 1939, but a 2,400-acre ranch with assorted pigs, horses, poultry, and sheep can be a very busy place. During shearing time each year, she would cook three meals a day for twenty-one shearers. Cooking began at 5:30 in the morning and Evelyn would do nothing but cook food and wash dishes until 8:30 at night. An entire pig would be cooked and eaten in three days. Visitors were frequent, but not always enthusiastically welcomed when there was so much work to be done.

Later, the family moved to Salt Lake City, where they lived for four years before moving to Murray, Utah, their home for another forty-six years. Evelyn did her quilting in a special room at the back of the house and almost always had a quilt on the frame. Ned had died in 1982, and in 1996 Evelyn moved to Bountiful, Utah, to be near her daughter, Louise. Her two sons live in Wyoming and Oregon.

Evelyn continued to quilt until her death, giving most of her creations away to family and friends. She missed the old house in Murray and her quilting room. She especially missed Ned's helping her prepare quilts for quilting.

Evelyn
Hoskisson
Nebeker

1937

Jacob's Ladder

67" x 89"

Cotton

Made by Evelyn Hoskisson Nebeker

(1908–1996)

Made at Connor Ranch, Daggett County,

Utah

Owned by Louise Gordon

Mary Alice (Mayme) Shaw Midgley

Quilting in this family is a tradition involving at least five generations. Elline Craig's grandmother and mother quilted, she quilts, her sister quilts, and some of her daughters and granddaughters quilt. The family has "good hands," as Elline's sister Jeanne Huber puts it.

Mary Alice Shaw's "good hands" led her to applique, quilting, and embroidery, all of which she did with three sisters who were equally talented. She was a pretty girl with a thick braided mane of strawberry red hair. In 1911, she married Rushby Midgley, a romantic, generous man for whom she had waited two years while he served a mission for the L.D.S. church in England. They settled in Salt Lake City, where they raised two sons and two daughters. Later, they moved to Bountiful, Utah, where Rushby had found land for a farm. Their grown children moved, too. Elline lived in a little farmhouse on the property, eventually building the home in which she and her husband still reside. Her brother built next door, her sister and parents up the street. There were orchards all around and streams and the quiet of the country.

Mary Alice appliqued the red and green blocks for this quilt in 1938, for her daughter Elline's trousseau. After sewing the blocks together, she drew the quilting designs onto the fabric and set the quilt on a frame, leaving it for Elline to quilt. She was on her way to be with her older daughter, Jeanne, who had just had a baby. Twenty-year-old Elline quilted between classes at the University of Utah, finishing before her mother returned home.

Elline calls this quilt pattern Leaf Applique, but it is also known as Wandering Foot. According to *The Romance of the Patchwork Quilt*, by Carrie Hall and Rose Kretsinger, the pattern had a curse associated with it in early America. No child was allowed to sleep under the pattern for fear he or she would grow up to be discontented or unstable or develop a desire to roam. No bride would have one in her trousseau. The name was eventually changed to Turkey Tracks. It is called Iris Leaf when it is done in green only on a white background.

Elline Craig has no memory of when she started quilting, but she has produced dozens of quilts, each one more intricate and beautiful than the last. There is a Yo-Yo quilt done in pink and blue prints, a stunning Whig Rose, an original green applique design she calls Falling Leaves, and a pattern she created to duplicate a mosaic floor she saw in Boston, a design she named The New Boston Commons. Several years ago she designed a red and green pineapple quilt that was featured in an article in a national quilting magazine and shown on the cover. She received dozens of letters from people all over the world who admired her quilt and wanted the pattern for it or were writing just to tell her how much they liked the design.

Elline prefers to do applique because it is less precise and a little more "forgiving" than piecing, although her stitches need no forgiveness. She does all the applique, piecing, and quilting in her lap without the aid of hoops. She uses a frame only for basting the quilt top, batting, and backing together before she begins quilting. Stipple quilting, which adds a wonderful texture to quilts, is one of Elline's favorite quilting techniques.

Elline's mother Mary Alice died in 1971 at the age of eighty-three. Remembering her mother, Elline often thinks of the ways that piecing and stitching can bring women together, even women who share no common language or culture. She remembers the time her mother taught a Maori woman from New Zealand how to quilt. Mere Whaanga came from her homeland in New Zealand to die and be buried next to her chieftain husband. She lived in a one-room apartment in Sugarhouse, a community south of Salt Lake City, with nothing to do to fill the long hours. Realizing how lonely the woman must be, Mary Alice visited her with offerings of fabric, needle and thread, compassion, and time. With many gestures and few words the two women learned to communicate, and Mere Whaanga learned how to hand piece a quilt top. She made dozens of them before her death, giving them to the Mormon missionaries she knew from New Zealand.

"The high prize of life," wrote Ralph Waldo Emerson, "the crowning fortune of a woman, is to be born with a bias to some pursuit which finds her in employment and happiness." For Elline Craig and her mother, the pursuit that led to their "high prize" was quilting.

1938

Leaf Applique

79" x 83½"

Cotton

Made by Mary Alice (Mayme) Shaw

Midgley (1889–1971) and

Elline Midgley Craig

Made in Salt Lake City, Salt Lake County,

Utah

Owned by Elline Midgley Craig

Maria
Vaughan
Austin

"Every stitch she made, she was thinking of me. Every time I see the quilt, I think of her," says Marguerite Orton of the charming wedding quilt made for her in 1938 by her grandmother Maria Vaughan Austin. Although it began as a kit, the quilt became an original as Maria added buttonhole stitching to each appliquéd piece and quilted the grid pattern in pink cotton crochet thread. She hand pieced the border from a bright mix of yellow, pink, green, and blue fabrics. The overall effect is both playful and sophisticated, a reflection of the quilt-maker that seems to say life can be serious, but it can also be a great deal of fun.

Maria Brain Vaughan was born in Lehi, Utah, in 1865. Her mother, Jane Maria Brain, had arrived in the Salt Lake Valley in 1861 with a handcart company. Michael Vaughan, her father, came from Wales. Maria was the oldest of their six children, all of whom were born and raised in Lehi. In 1887 Maria married Mark Austin, an English immigrant whose family had also settled in Lehi. Mark worked for the Utah-Idaho Sugar Company, first as a field supervisor and then as a general superintendent. His work caused the family to move often, leaving Lehi in 1909 to live subsequently in Colorado, Salt Lake City, and Idaho. The family moved permanently to Salt Lake City in the 1930s. Maria and Mark had seven children; their second child, Jane, died when she was a year old.

Maria worked hard in her home no matter where it was, striving to make it an attractive and comfortable haven for her family and the many people they entertained because of Mark's job. She filled her home with crocheting, knitting, crewel work, needlepoint, quilting, and anything else that interested her. She produced many original designs and embellishments to satisfy her creativity. When Marguerite was sixteen, her grandmother made her a pair of gloves with Irish crochet that were "the envy of all the girls." Maria had always been fashionably well groomed and well mannered, although she could handle a team of horses with the best of them or drive a car, which she owned from the day they first became available. She stood only five feet tall, her petite frame disguising the self-reliant, independent woman within.

Marguerite remembers her grandmother as an excellent teacher, working with young people even into her eighties. Maria taught Marguerite many of the hand skills she enjoys today. The cheerful quilt she made to celebrate her granddaughter's marriage more than fifty years ago is still aglow with the warm and loving personality of its maker.

1938

Floral Applique

73" x 89"

Cotton

Made by Maria Vaughan Austin

(1865–1950)

Made in Salt Lake City, Salt Lake County,

Utah

Owned by Marguerite Orton

Lydia Rowbury Coulson

The road to Castle Dale in Emery County, Utah, was long and dusty that December day in 1901. Jesse Coulson and Lydia Rowbury were traveling by buckboard to find a justice of the peace to marry them. They had been courting for several years, and a mutual acquaintance had suggested it was "high time" they got married. Also in the buckboard were Lydia's aunt Elizabeth Jewkes Rowbury and her cousin Eric Rowbury. After the four o'clock ceremony, the wedding party returned to Huntington, Utah, where Lydia had been living with her aunt and uncle. Jesse stayed there for a short time before returning to his home in Nephi, Utah. Lydia remained in Huntington. In the spring, Lydia joined her husband in Nephi, where she would live the rest of her life and bring up her two children.

Lydia Rowbury was born in England to Ann Bissell and William Erastus Rowbury, the oldest of six children. The family came to Utah when Lydia was five years old, settling in Sanpete County. Lydia was ten years old when her mother died and she was sent to live with relatives. Her life with Jesse in Nephi began with a homestead known as Marsh Flat in Nephi Canyon, located five miles from town, where yellow roses and tamarack still grow. Shortly after their marriage, Jesse's sister Elizabeth Cole died, leaving three children, Ruby, Dave, and Emma. Ruby was sent to live with her Grandmother Cole, and Lydia and Jesse became parents to the younger children. That wasn't always an easy task, especially when Dave would take little Emma to town with the horse and buggy, and Lydia would have to walk the five miles in search of them.

Eventually, the Coulsons moved into Nephi, to an adobe house known as the old Jenkins place. It had two rooms, each measuring fourteen feet by sixteen feet with twelve-foot ceilings, and two lean-to rooms. Jesse continued to work in the canyon hauling firewood as well as at the salt spring. Lydia had achieved a fifth-grade education, but Jesse, who had no schooling, worked all his life as a laborer. They also kept a couple of cows and a few chickens; Lydia churned butter and had eggs to sell.

In 1915, after thirteen years of marriage, Lydia and Jesse became parents to a daughter. They named her Anna. When she was five years old, her brother Jesse was born. By then, Lydia was almost forty years old.

Anna remembers that she never had a store-bought dress until she graduated from high school. Lydia was an excellent seamstress and quilter, earning three dollars to quilt for others during the Great Depression. Lydia had always told Anna that she would never cut new fabric to make a quilt top—that is, until she saw the Improved Nine-patch pattern. Anna bought the "slip sheen" fabric for her mother, and Lydia set to work.

The pastel blue, pink, and yellow pieces are machine pieced and hand quilted in eight even stitches to the inch. Lydia always did her own quilting, fearing that a group of quilters would make stitches "big enough to catch your toenails in." Most of the quilting is done "in the ditch" (stitches quilted close to the seam rather than the customary quarter inch away), but there is also a petal design quilted in blue thread in each of the blue pieces. The edges are finished in a scallop to accentuate the shape of the sashing and border.

Lydia Rowbury Coulson died in 1950 at the age of sixty-nine. She left behind only three of her beautiful quilts, all in the possession of her daughter Anna: a purple Star, a Double Wedding Ring, and the Improved Nine-patch.

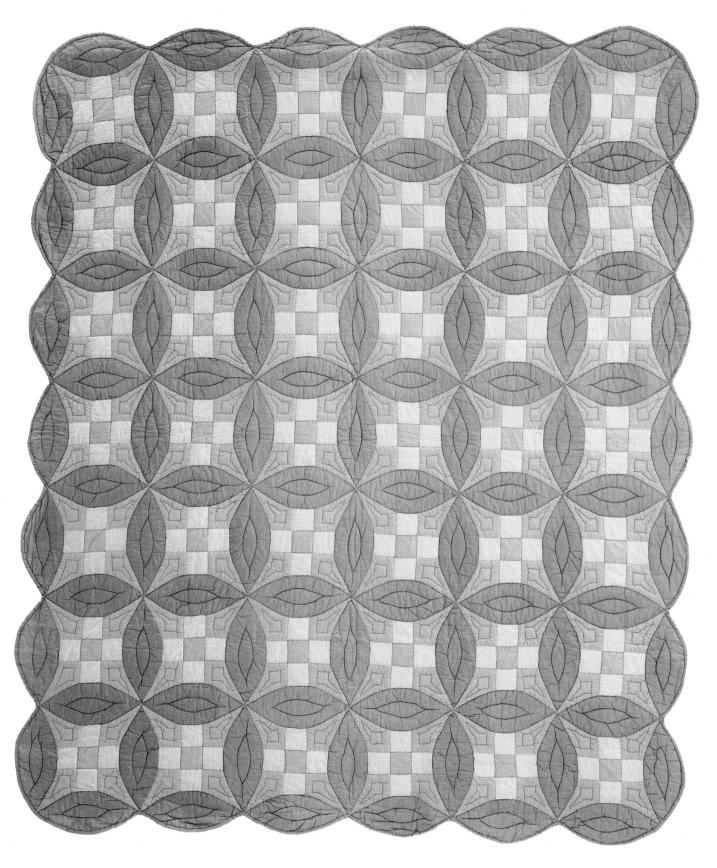

Late 1930s

Improved Nine-patch

76½" x 91"

Glazed or Polished Cotton ("Slip Sheen")

Made by Lydia Rowbury Coulson

(1881–1950)

Made in Nephi, Juab County, Utah

Owned by Anna Coulson Embry

Mayme
Pargis

Lynndyl, Utah, was created in 1904 on the main line of the Union Pacific Railroad as a divisional point on the route from Salt Lake City to Los Angeles, where engineers and brakemen stopped to make repairs on their iron horses and conductors hurried to fill their empty stomachs at The Beanery before the train pulled out. Families lived in Lynndyl, but it was a temporary place for most, a town with a history of coming and going, pulling in and pulling out, repairing and moving on, a transient place where many came but few remained. When the trains stopped coming in the 1950s, Lynndyl had to find a new identity.

The Banks family lived in Lynndyl during its heyday. James Alma Banks, his wife, Gladys, and their six children established a loving home in the railroad town, working hard to make it a place of permanence in the mobile atmosphere of the little central Utah community. Alma was the bishop of the Lynndyl L.D.S. Ward for ten years, also working as a section hand for the railroad. Gladys and her sister Winnie had been two of the first women editors of a newspaper in the United States, the *Panguitch Progress*. Gladys was a former schoolteacher, who valued education and lived to see three of her children receive college degrees.

During the 1920s, a railroad worker named Joe Pargis and his wife, Mayme, were transferred to Lynndyl from the Union Pacific Railroad's headquarters in Omaha. Joe was later injured in a boiler accident in Lynndyl and received a substantial settlement from the railroad. He and Mayme remained in Lynndyl, where Joe became a "free-lance banker," lending money to those

he deemed trustworthy and collecting, with interest, on payday. He was shorter than his wife, a stocky man with a thick accent. Children were intimidated by him, but he was well respected by the adults in town. The Banks children delivered the newspaper to the Pargis home, each one in turn as they reached the appropriate age. Whenever she collected the monthly bill, quilt owner Ruth Banks Abegglen remembers that Mayme and Joe always invited her into their home for a treat.

Mayme was not a member of the L.D.S. church, but she went to Relief Society meetings faithfully, both for the company and for the quilting. She was an exceptional quilter, making beautiful scrap Star quilt tops for both Ruth and her younger sister, Gladys. She also loved to crochet and do other needle-work. Ruth's brother Wayne remembers her handmade shawls hanging everywhere in the house. She was a gracious and friendly neighbor to everyone.

When Ruth was married in 1943, Mayme gave her this beautiful Lone Star quilt top as a gift. It was quilted later by the Lynndyl Relief Society. The center of the star radiates in color from white to gray to yellow to pink; the colors of the star points move inward in the opposite order. The scrapbag prints and solids are a delightful assortment of fabrics Mayme gathered over the years. Her balanced, artful arrangement of the tiny diamond-shaped pieces creates a very pleasant design. Ruth's sister Gladys has a quilt top almost identical to Ruth's that Mayme gave her in 1954 when Gladys returned from a L.D.S. mission. The two sisters did not realize that each had a quilt made by Mayme until the Utah Quilt Heritage Corporation began research on Ruth's quilt.

Joe died in Lynndyl, where he is buried. Mayme returned to her birthplace in Iowa, where Gladys visited her in the late 1950s. She was nearly blind and no longer able to produce her beautiful handwork. Mayme died in Columbus City, Iowa, at ninety years of age.

1940s

Lone Star

68½" x 75"

Cotton

Made by Mayme Pargis (1872–1962)

Made in Lynndyl, Millard County, Utah

Owned by Ruth Abegglen

Ida
Victoria
Jensen
Childs

Gunnison, Utah, was created in 1862 from two temporary settlements that had been established in 1859 on the lower Sanpitch River. When Brigham Young visited the two communities in 1862, he described their swampy location as "too muddy for a hog's wallow" and recommended that they combine and move the two towns onto the higher bench area of the surrounding hills. The new town was named for Captain John Gunnison, a government explorer who had been killed by Indians in the Sevier Valley in 1853.

By combining two unprofitable settlements into one, the settlers soon saw an increase in their fortunes. A sawmill was built in 1863 and a black-smith shop added in 1867. The population increased that same year when a number of settlers were driven from the Sevier County colonies by Indian difficulties and permanently relocated in Gunnison. Agriculture thrived in the irrigated farmlands, and sugar beets became an important export crop. When the railroad came to Gunnison in the late 1800s, the population more than doubled.

Rasmus Jensen came to Gunnison sometime before 1867. He had immigrated from his native Denmark, one of the nearly 17,000 Danes to join the L.D.S. church and "gather in Zion" in the nineteenth century. In 1866, he married Ingar Hansen, a Swedish convert to the church who was three years his senior. The couple had five children, two of whom died as babies.

Gunnison was the American home of Rasmus and Ingar for the remainder of their lives. Their oldest child, Ida Victoria, who was born in the little pioneer town in 1867, also lived there until her death in 1958. When she was seventeen, she married twenty-six-year-old Lorenzo Howard Childs of Kaysville, Utah. They lived and farmed in Gunnison and raised four children to adulthood; one daughter had died as a child and a baby was stillborn.

Ida quilted for her children until she was past eighty years of age. The Double X quilt owned by her grand-daughter Gertrude Beck typifies her quilting style. It is constructed from sewing scraps carefully machine pieced into a Nine-patch design. The blocks are set together with salmon-colored sashing connected with three-inch-square green posts. The defining feature of this quilt, and the trait that distin-guishes it as one made by Ida, is the backing fabric. It is made from five-and ten-pound muslin salt sacks that were unstitched, then sewn together and dyed in a solution of copperas and lye that resulted in an orange-gold color. Gertrude recalls that her grandmother used this procedure in making the back of every quilt she stitched. The batting is wool, and the layers are quilted around the post pieces and diagonally through each of the small squares.

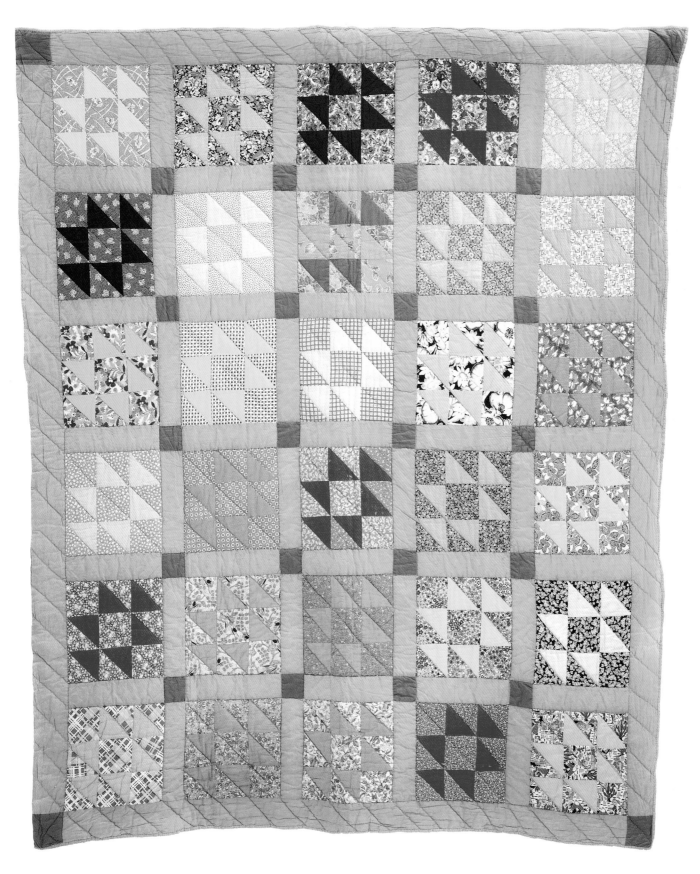

1940s

Double X

72″ x 88″

Cotton

Made by Ida Victoria Jensen Childs

(1867–1958)

Made in Gunnison, Sanpete County, Utah

Owned by Gertrude Beck

Zilphia Smith first met John Franson when she was a young girl visiting in Oakley, Utah, with her mother. Before he settled in the Kamas Valley in the 1880s, Johnny had come from Sweden, the birthplace of Zilphia's mother, working his way westward on the railroad. Zilphia and John were married in Peoa, Utah, on July 24, 1885.

The Kamas Valley lies eighteen miles east of Park City, Utah. It was first described in 1849 by Captain Howard Stansbury as a prairie consisting "of most excellent land. . . . Water for stock is abundant and timber for ordinary farming is plentiful and convenient." Thomas Rhoades was the original settler in the valley, coming in 1859 with twenty Mormon families. Peoa, which is fifteen miles north of Kamas at the base of present-day Rockport Reservoir, had been settled by a small group of pioneers in 1857 who did not stay there through the winter, returning in 1860 to build a permanent settlement.

Scandinavian Latter-day Saints began moving from Salt Lake City to Peoa in 1863 when they were advised by Brigham Young to settle "in the higher country like where you came from, where there is plenty of wood for buildings and homes, good water and land for your livestock, and space to raise your families." The first settlement one mile south of Peoa near a bend of the Weber River was known as "Woodenshoe" because of the wooden shoes customarily worn by the people. The large Scandinavian population drew John and Zilphia to the Kamas Valley.

John and Zilphia became farmers in Oakley, located halfway between Kamas and Peoa, where they spent their married years raising eight children. Sometimes the crops were good, sometimes they failed, and the weather often seemed to have an agenda all its own. Children and animals got sick, and everyone had to be fed. There was bread to make, fruit to bottle, and choke-cherries to boil into jelly. And there was quilting. Zilphia always had a quilt on the frame, always piecing or stitching another creation to keep the family warm or to give as a wedding gift.

When her nephew Steven Johnson was married in 1941, she gave the new couple this delicate pink quilt. She was seventy-seven years old. Roma Johnson remembers Zilphia using a teacup to trace the clamshell design she quilted into the eighteen-inch border. The medallion design is an original, with beautifully appliqued petals and leaves stitched with silk thread. The vines, stems, and baskets are skillfully embroidered, highlighted by Zilphia's even stitching in the quilted grid surrounding them.

Zilphia continued quilting into her eighties, designing and producing with her usual flair.

1941

Pink Floral

81¾" x 87½"

Satin

Made by Zilphia Smith Franson

(1864–1951)

Made in Oakley, Summit County, Utah

Owned by Roma Johnson

Mary Cotter went to a Salt Lake City swap meet in May of 1989 looking for an old quilt in good condition, something beautiful but simple with a story to tell. When she left, she was the owner of an intricately embroidered Friendship/ Album quilt apparently stitched by members of the twenty-three Rebekah Lodges of Utah. The quilt was constructed of twenty-seven blocks including a central medallion bordered on each side with a rectangular piece on which were embroidered three intertwined chain links. Four embroidered symbols were repeated on the blocks: a beehive, a dove, a lily, and a new moon with seven stars. One square supplied a documented date: "Bee Hive Rebekah Lodge No. 34, Payson, 1942." But Mary knew nothing additional about the quilt, nor did the seller. She was determined to learn more.

The *World Book Encyclopedia* informed Mary that the Rebekah Lodge is the International Association of Rebekah Assemblies, the women's auxiliary of the Independent Order of Odd Fellows (I.O.O.F.), a large fraternal and benevolent order. In 1995 the national membership was 500,000. It was founded in England, probably in the early 1700s, but the American organization separated in 1843 from the British parent order. In 1851, the Rebekah Degree, or Lodge, was adopted so that women could be admitted into the Order. On the Great Seal of the Odd Fellow is emblazoned, "We command you to visit the sick, relieve the distressed, bury the dead and educate the orphan." In adherence to this direction, the I.O.O.F. gives aid, assistance, and comfort to its members and their families; sponsors financial aid to college students; and maintains homes for the aged, the indigent, and widows and orphans.

Because of the inscription embroidered on the center block of the quilt—the words "SMILE AND SERVE, Wasatch 30, Sandy" stitched beneath a glowing rainbow—Mary contacted the Rebekah Lodge in Sandy, Utah. She spoke with Geneva Lewis, a longtime member who recalled that in 1942 and 1943 her aunt Marie Grow Stewart had served as president of the Sandy Lodge. Her personal symbol was a rainbow. Perhaps, she suggested, the quilt had been made under President Stewart's leadership to be raffled off for fund-raising. Or it may have been made as a presentation quilt for Marie Stewart from the twenty-three Rebekah Lodges in Utah. It appears that each lodge in Utah contributed a block to the quilt.

Whatever the reason for its creation, the Rebekah quilt is a carefully thought out, well-planned design. All motifs were traced from the same template onto white fabric, then embroidered and embellished by the individual block makers. The doves are especially beautiful, each one sewn with white six-strand floss on white fabric. The three intertwined links bordering the rainbow represent friendship, love, and truth. The beehive and lily symbols, significant to the Rebekah Lodges, have been meaningful to Utahns, too, since the 1800s. The light pink sashing and the light green backing used in the quilt are Rebekah Lodge colors.

As of 1989, there were eleven Rebekah Lodges in Utah—six in the Salt Lake Valley, two in Ogden, and one each in Corinne, Delta, and Milford.

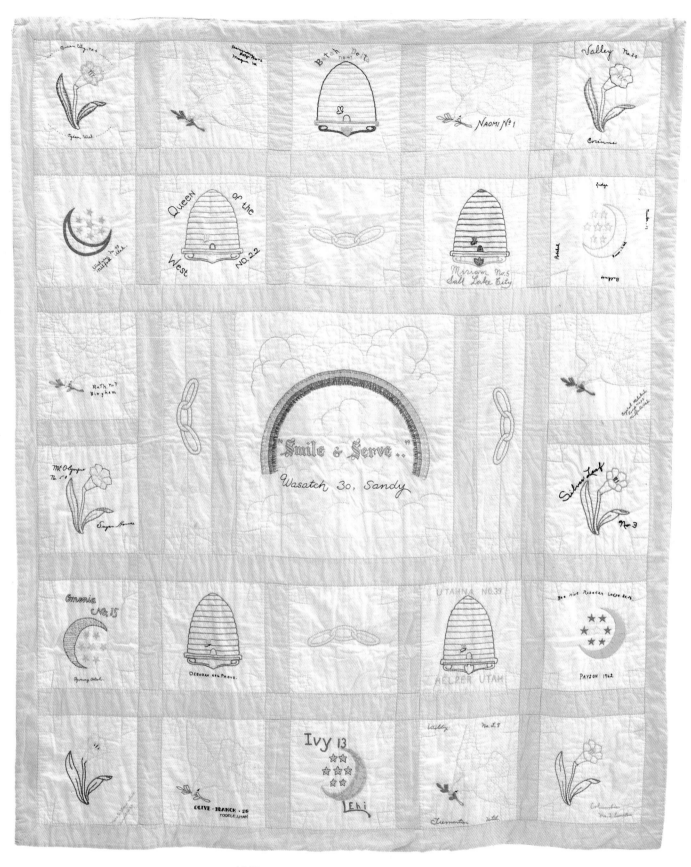

1942

Friendship/Album Quilt

65" x 77"

Cotton

Made by Rebekah Lodges of Utah

Made in twenty-three Utah towns

Owned by Mary Cotter

Mary
Hazel
Norr
Jorgensen

The Indian Wedding Ring is a well-known variation of the popular Double Wedding Ring quilt pattern. The Double Wedding Ring is usually worked from a scrap-bag palette of colors on a light background; and it is the circles you notice, calico circles linked in an eternal round with other calico circles, appearing to extend forever across the surface of the quilt. But in Hazel Jorgensen's Indian Wedding Ring quilt, done in white and gold, it is the stylized central diamond shape that stands out. The circles are there, pieced from tiny white and gold diamonds, but they accentuate the larger golden shapes that beat like a drum as the eye scans the rhythm of the quilt.

Hazel Jorgensen was a quilter of the highest caliber. "I love to quilt," she wrote in 1976, "and enjoyed making quilts for the girls when they were married. As the grandchildren were getting older, I had a great desire to make a quilt . . . for each one of them." The Indian Wedding Ring quilt was made in 1942 for Hazel's oldest daughter, Dorothy. Hazel did make a quilt for each of her twelve grand-children, and an extra one so the last grandchild to be married would have a choice. Hazel was also skilled in fine embroidery and was commissioned in the 1950s to fashion a flag with the United Nations' symbol on both sides, which was presented to Governor J. Bracken Lee.

Mary Hazel Norr was born January 10, 1896, in Idaho to Olef James and Mary Harris Norr, the sixth of their eight children. When she was five years old, the family moved to Logan, Utah (for better schooling). Her childhood

was a happy time of school and friends and church. She sang in an L.D.S. church choir for five years, recalling that the leader August Hansen would enthusiastically admonish his choir members to sing with "wim and wigor." Hazel was working as a telephone operator when the good news came of the end of World War I. On November 20, 1918, she recorded, "I must tell of the night we received the news that Germany had surrendered. It came about 1:30 A.M. . . . . The bells and whistles were heard constantly until the following day."

In 1920 Hazel married Ariel Jorgensen, a boy she had known at school. She moved with Ariel to his farm in Amalga, a very small town outside of Logan, where they lived in a small log cabin with a front room, kitchen, and porch. Ariel had covered the living room walls with oilcloth, making it "very cheery." Their first daughter, Dorothy, was born there in 1921, and their second daughter, Carol, in 1923. Two years later the family moved into a new home that Ariel had designed and built. Maxine, their third daughter, was born there in 1929.

Hazel's life was plunged into despair when nine-year-old Carol drowned in 1933. She wrote that a close friend counseled her that "some day it will seem like a sad, sweet memory. But I thought I would never be happy again." Ten years later, there was great joy in her life when Dorothy gave birth to triplet boys, Hazel's first grand-children. They lived with Hazel and Ariel the first ten months of their lives, bringing peace and consolation to her heart.

Without warning, sixty-three-year-old Hazel suffered a small stroke in February 1959, and was soon paralyzed from the waist down. After three

months of intensive therapy, Hazel was able to get around once again with the aid of crutches and a wheelchair, which she used for the rest of her life. True to form, she continued to quilt and to travel with Ariel.

When Ariel died in October 1969, Hazel wrote of the loss of "my best friend, my wonderful husband and life companion." She considered it "the saddest thing that has ever come to me in my whole life."

Sherrie Kasteler now owns her Grandma Jorgensen's elegant Indian Wedding Ring quilt. The positive legacy Hazel left is evident when Sherrie describes Hazel's reaction to her paralysis: "How grateful I was," she often told her family, "to still have my arms and hands."

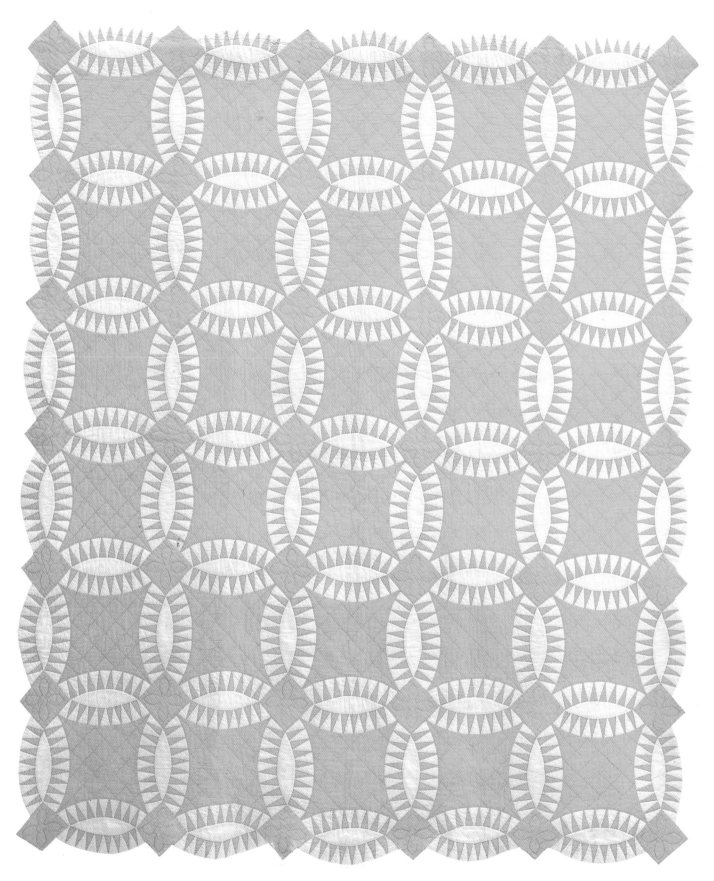

1942

Indian Wedding Ring

71″ x 85″

Cotton

Made by Mary Hazel Norr Jorgensen

(1896–1987)

Made in Amalga, Cache County, Utah

Owned by Sherrie Kasteler

Lois Roberts was nine years old when her brother Blaine was born. It was a memorable day because it was also the day her father, Frank Roberts, died. Badly injured in a mining accident, he had held on to life just long enough to learn of the birth of his last child. The baby was two weeks old before Lois's mother, Jane, was strong enough to be told about her husband's death.

Life changed dramatically for the Roberts family that April 5, 1895. With six fatherless children ranging in age from newborn to eleven years, something had to be done to make a living. Childhood ended for Lois and her older sister, Inez, when they were forced to find jobs. Nine-year-old Lois found work washing dishes in a restaurant in Minersville, Utah. She was too little to reach the sink without standing on a wooden box.

For the next eight years Lois worked at one job or another to help her mother feed and clothe the family. At seventeen, she married Andrew Jackson Hollingshead, a carpenter. Getting married, however, wasn't as easy as it was to plan. With two wagons and two other couples they set out in the early winter of 1902 for the St. George L.D.S. Temple. During the night before they were to be married, they were caught in a flash flood that carried one wagon downstream, damaging the boys' clothes and supplies beyond repair. The girls' wagon was spared, so they were beautifully dressed for their weddings on November 12.

Lois and Andrew settled in Minersville, where they raised five children, having one son die as an infant. Their only girl and the youngest child was named Joy for the elation Lois felt in finally having a daughter. The California Poppy quilt belongs to her. Joy owns a beautiful Lancaster Rose quilt also made by her mother. Although it is exquisitely beautiful, Joy remembers sleeping beneath it as a child because her mother made it to be used. Lois always had a quilt on a frame that could be raised to the ceiling on pulleys if the room was needed. Christmas was the only time the frame was put away so Lois could hang garlands and a paper bell from the light in the center of the ceiling.

The California Poppy is a wholecloth appliqued quilt with decorative stitching in the poppy centers and on the leaves. The subtly scalloped white background of the quilt is an excellent showcase for Lois's artful hand quilting, which is done in feather and flower motifs and a grid. Lois chose the poppy pattern because Joy had recently moved to California. The quilt has never been used or washed, treasured instead as a keepsake.

Lois Hollingshead quilted well into her eighties and managed to make at least one quilt for every year of her long life.

Lois
Adelaide
Roberts
Hollingshead

1943

California Poppy

74″ x 84″

Cotton

Made by Lois Adelaide Roberts
Hollingshead (1885–1980)
Made in Minersville, Beaver County, Utah
Owned by Joy Hollingshead Kirk

Blenda Snow was born in Ferron, Utah, one of the most landlocked places in North America, hundreds of miles from the Pacific Ocean and thousands of miles from the Atlantic—a western desert town, where the women watched their men go off to farm or herd cattle, but never to watch them sail off in a whaling ship, praying for their safe return. And yet, when she was fifty-five years old, Blenda Snow sat in her farmhouse in south-central Utah and stitched a masterpiece: a blue and white Mariner's Compass quilt that is both as tranquil and serene as a calm day on the ocean and perfect as a memorial for a son or a husband or a father lost to the sea.

The Mariner's Compass pattern can be traced to Mediterranean sailors who used eight predictable winds to navigate by. These winds were shown on maps and charts by a design called a wind rose. Eventually, the magnetic compass replaced using the winds in navigating. A drawing of the compass was placed over the wind rose on maps, and the combined image became known as a compass rose. Executed in fabric as a quilt pattern, the compass rose became known as the Mariner's Compass.

Although Blenda never called her quilt pattern by this name, her rendition of the compass is flawless. The thirty-eight-inch central medallion has thirty-two points, which qualifies it as a true Mariner's Compass. Her skill is evident in each smooth, precise point; there is no puckering or straining as the points rotate around the perfect central circle. The quilting is equally impressive. Clamshell designs cover the white interior of the quilt while a cable pattern weaves in and out of the border. Each of the pieced shapes has been outlined with quilting. The small white stitches are especially beautiful to see against the blue backing of the quilt.

Blenda Snow was born in Ferron on October 7, 1889, to John Heber and Ida Hansen Ralphs. She was a farmer's daughter who became a farmer's wife when she married Clifford Snow in 1909. They worked hard to make a meager living as they raised their three children—two sons and a daughter. Blenda was a prolific quilter in her spare time, making at least thirty quilts for her children and grandchildren. It is difficult to imagine that any of those quilts could surpass the artistry of the Mariner's Compass she gave to her granddaughter Ann.

Blenda
Ralphs
Snow

1944

Mariner's Compass

72" x 86"

Cotton

Made by Blenda Ralphs Snow

(1889–1959)

Made in Ferron, Emery County, Utah

Owned by Ann Marshall

Irene Mangelson

There are two things Irene Mangelson would change about her Postage Stamp quilt if she could: the center square and the backing. "I never liked the color of the center piece," she says, "and fabric for the back was so hard to get during the war, we just took what we could find. But I was never satisfied with the quality of the material."

Color and quality were the chief concerns of seventeen-year-old Irene as she set out to reproduce the quilt her great-grandmother had made in England between 1840 and 1890.

She and her twin sister, Jeane, had seen the quilt during a visit to their aunt's home in Salt Lake and challenged each other to copy it. Fifteen months and 11,605 pieces later, Irene was the undisputed champion. It took three years' work for Jeane to finish her patchwork quilt.

A fire at Juab High School during Irene's senior year provided her with the chance to work on her tiny fabric squares almost daily. The Levan students were bused to Nephi, Utah, where their classes were held in the long unused rooms of a vacant building. Irene would sit in the back of the room with a matchbox full of fabric and square paper shapes and stitch the afternoons away. In the evenings she would sew the pieces into longer strips, then sew those strips to others she had completed.

The technique Irene used in making this quilt is called "English paper piecing." The three-quarter-inch shapes are traced onto stiff paper using a brass template, and the fabric is cut into small squares just enough larger to allow the edges to be folded over the paper and basted into place. The tiny blocks are then whipstitched together

and the paper is later torn away. Irene left the paper liners in her blocks until the entire quilt top was stitched together; it took her two weeks of constant work to remove the papers.

Irene quilted outward from the center of the quilt using a chain motif at about four stitches per inch. One of the quilt's most outstanding features is the finished edge, with its hundreds of tiny jagged points. Equally striking is the arrangement of colors in this Trip Around the World pattern. It draws the eyes outward as they focus on each of the tiny colored chips in every shade of red, yellow, blue, violet, and green.

Irene's exquisite miniature patchwork took first place in the Juab County Fair in 1947, the year after her marriage to Golden Mangelson. Their five children grew up surrounded by scraps and thimbles, needles and thread. To date, Irene has made more than 150 quilts. Each of her grandchildren receives a quilt upon graduation from high school. She is also the quilting director for her L.D.S. ward in Levan, and oversees the completion of seven or eight quilts a year. She quilts professionally for women in Salt Lake City, too, and manages to do a little quilting for herself.

Postage Stamp quilts like Irene's were especially popular during the 1920s and 1930s because the stamp-sized pieces, which typically measured one square inch, could be easily gathered from the scrapbag. An elegant Burgoyne Surrounded or an Irish Chain quilt stitched from salvaged fabrics in the midst of the Great Depression brought beauty and warmth into many struggling households. Irene's more contemporary rendition is a marvelous illustration of a genre that requires patient and persistent piecing.

Detail
Boston Commons
Made by Gertrude Esposito Yarmer
Owned by Claudia Crump

Burgoyne Surrounded
Made by Minnie Petersen Jorgensen
Owned by Sherrie Kasteler

1944–1945

Postage Stamp

71″ x 80″

Cotton

Made and owned by Irene Mangelson

(1926–)

Made in Levan, Juab County, Utah

Minnie
May
Bowns
Cox

Minnie May Cox had a quilting room in the back of her home in Woodruff, Utah. For most of the year, a quilt of one design or another sat on the frame, waiting for her quick fingers to stitch around the outlines of the shapes she had carefully pieced. When winter set in, the frame stood empty because Minnie's fingers were too cold and stiff in the unheated room to work a needle through the layers of fabric and batting. Springtime meant more quilting on a top or two pieced during the long, snowy months.

Minnie May loved quilting, whether it was to keep her family warm or to give as a gift, whether it was sewing a simple camp quilt made from worn-out overalls or piecing an unusual design like the Six-pointed Stars. Quilting was an extension of her considerable talent as a seamstress. She made most of the clothing for her eight children by hand and often used the scraps to fashion quilt tops. Her daughters learned to sew when they were children, just as she had learned to sew, crochet, embroider, and knit from her own mother. Her oldest daughter, Inge, became a professional dressmaker.

Life began for Minnie in the small mining settlement of Almy, Wyoming, five miles northwest of Evanston. She was the fifth of eight children born to James and Christina Spowart Bowns. At the time of her birth in 1881, the three oldest Bowns children had died, leaving only Minnie and her older sister, Teenie. Another son was born when Minnie was two years old, and a daughter two years later who died when she was five. Minnie's parents took in boarders who worked in the nearby coal mines, and the children learned to cook and clean early in their lives. Minnie probably charmed many of the lonely miners with her deep-set blue eyes and her cheerful demeanor.

In 1899, Minnie married Jacob Soren Hemple in the Salt Lake L.D.S. Temple. They had three little girls, Inge, May, and Lillian. Jacob died in 1907, and Minnie and her daughters moved back to Almy to live with her parents. She was twenty-six years old.

Minnie remained close to her sister, Teenie, who had married Heber Cox, often visiting them in their home in Woodruff, which they shared with Heber's father, John, and his unmarried brother, William. Four years after Jacob's death, Minnie married William Cox and settled in Woodruff. Five children were born to them, a pair of twin boys named Emerson and Lynn, two daughters named Annie and Millicent, and a son named Lavaun.

Life in Woodruff was life on the frontier. Drinking water was drawn from an open well, culinary water from a creek west of the house. Laundry was washed by hand in a tub with a washboard. The bathroom was "the best outdoor plumbing money could buy." Minnie milked cows, made butter, and raised chickens. She taught her children to work hard, make the best of what they had, and complain as little as possible. She taught her sons to respect and honor women, often telling them that "women were the highest of God's creations." She also taught her children to love books through example, for she read anything she could get her hands on.

Minnie made the Six-pointed Stars quilt for her son, Lavaun, and his bride, Zella, when they married in 1945. Lavaun was in the service, and Minnie would tell Zella about the carefully planned quilt as she made it. The top was hand pieced, even though Minnie owned a treadle sewing machine. The fabric was probably purchased at the Golden Rule Store in Evanston, Wyoming, the nearest "big city" to Woodruff. The quilt construction is unique in that the blocks are square rather than hexagonal.

1945

Six-pointed Stars

81½″ x 85½″

Cotton

Made by Minnie May Bowns Cox

(1881–1959)

Made in Woodruff, Rich County, Utah

Owned by Zella and Lavaun Cox

Emeline Cox Jewkes

It is easy to guess how this popular quilt pattern got its name. In a humorous parody of the muddled, dizzying trail of a drunkard on his way home from the tavern, the design starts and stops and weaves across the surface of the quilt. Although it appears complicated, the pattern is actually made from simple two-patch pieces: squares with a quarter circle cut from one corner. It is pieced using light and dark fabrics—usually red and white—which are interchanged in the blocks. Best known as The Drunkard's Path, the same arrangement of squares is also known as Rocky Road to Dublin, Rocky Road to California (after 1849), Country Husband, and Falling Timber. In Salem, Ohio, the pattern was known as Robbing Peter to Pay Paul. Other variations using different arrangements of the same pattern shapes are known as Love Ring, Nonesuch, Fool's Puzzle, Wonder of the World, Around the World, Vine of Friendship, and Pumpkin Vine.

Emeline Jewkes used the classic red and white color arrangement in her Drunkard's Path, with just a slight twist. The red fabric is a medium floral print mixed with green, a combination that gives the quilt a light and delicate appearance. The squares are machine pieced and quilted in red, with seven even stitches to the inch, and framed with red floral and white borders. Emeline made the quilt in 1946 as a wedding gift for her eighth child and third daughter, Beth Jewkes. It was only one of dozens of quilts she made during her eighty-seven years of life.

Emeline Cox was born in 1887 to Mary Ellen Parry and Sylvester Hulet Cox in the farming town of Orangeville, Utah, three miles from Castle Dale in Emery County. Orangeville was known as Upper Castle Dale until 1882, when it took a new name in honor of Orange Seely, who was the L.D.S. bishop of the entire region east of the Wasatch Plateau. According to the *Utah History Encyclopedia*,* Bishop Seely was an enormous man who made his benevolent rounds riding one mule, leading another mule behind him loaded with food, blacksmith tools, and dental forceps. He could shoe horses, sharpen plowshares, and remove teeth as needed.

The Cox family had originally settled in Manti, Utah, in 1852, led by Emeline's grandfather, Fredrick Walter Cox. Population growth and increasing livestock herds in central Utah probably led them to answer a call issued by Brigham Young in August 1877 for Castle Valley settlers. By 1880, 237 people were homesteading along a six-mile stretch of Cottonwood Creek, including Emeline's parents who married in December of that year.

Emeline was the fourth of the eleven children born to Sylvester and Mary Cox and their first daughter. Her mother taught her how to piece and applique quilts and take tiny, even stitches. She taught her own three daughters the same skills, although she always seemed to surpass them in talent and patience. Whenever Beth made a quilt, she asked her mother to draw the pattern and help with the piecing, then together they quilted the top, often with one of her sisters.

When Emeline was eighteen years old, she married Alma Gardiner Jewkes, a widower with three small children. Together, they had ten more children, five of whom are still living. The oldest child, Fred Jewkes, remembers his mother as an even-tempered, good-natured woman who raised children and flowers. Out of necessity, she always planted a wonderful vegetable garden to feed her hungry brood, but she could never turn away a traveling salesman. Once, after promising Fred and his wife that she would never buy another useless item from another peddler, she bought a can opener, paying for her purchase through a small hole in the screen door to make the deed less conspicuous.

Emeline Cox Jewkes died in 1974 at the age of eighty-seven. Her son-in-law Morris Huntington now owns the whimsical Drunkard's Path quilt she gave him and her daughter Beth for their wedding. Beth died in April 1995. The quilt is a touching reminder of the beauty she and her mother created while they were alive.

*Edited by Allan Kent Powell, published by the University of Utah Press, Salt Lake City, ©1994.

1946

Drunkard's Path

75" x 92"

Cotton

Made by Emeline Cox Jewkes

(1887–1974)

Made in Castle Dale, Emery County, Utah

Owned by Morris Huntington

Ruth
Delila
Kiesel
Jensen

Ruth Jensen had a great deal in common with her maternal grandmother, Johanna Petersen. Like her frugal Danish grandmother, she was a tireless worker, devoting long hours to her home and family. Also like her grandmother, who had lost two babies in infancy, Ruth buried four of her own six children. And like Johanna, who spun and wove wool into fine fabric for handmade clothes and quilts, Ruth was a quiltmaker of the highest order. Her daughter Dorothy owns a collection of fifty quilts made by Ruth, each one a fascinating creation, each one a showcase for the tiny stitches and meticulous handwork she perfected through the years. In a journal written when she was eighty-two years old, she wrote simply that quilting was her "main hobby," but it was apparently much more than that.

Ruth's mother and grandparents had come from Denmark in 1884, settling in Manti, Utah, where her grandfather Peter had found work. They were Mormon converts of only a year and were eager to "gather with the Saints" in Utah. Ruth was born in Manti thirteen years later, the second child of Christine Petersen and George Christian Kiesel. There were eleven Kiesel children, seven boys and four girls. Ruth became the oldest child when her brother Ray died nine days before his third birthday.

Her childhood was filled with days spent with Grandma Petersen, who lived four blocks away. Grandmother Petersen was a pleasant person and Ruth loved to be with her. "She was full of nonsense and could always make you laugh and feel better." She was a wonderful cook, too. Her cream pies were a favorite of Ruth's, as was the dumpling soup she cooked in a round, black pot. Bread was always baked in round loaves with buttered crusts. A glass bowl of fresh fruit sat on a table, sometimes filled with black currants that grew by the south fence of the property. Ruth remembered her grandmother milking cows that were "so big and fat, there was hardly room for Grandma to be in the stall." She often watched Johanna "sitting in the kitchen spinning yarn or carding wool."

Ruth's childhood was also filled with hard work. "Mother's health was poor," she wrote, "so a lot of the responsibility fell on me, being the oldest and four boys right after me. I learned what hard work was." Laundry day was especially strenuous. Clothes were scrubbed on a washboard. White clothes were boiled in a big black tub over an open fire or in the kitchen. After boiling, the clothes were plucked from the hot suds with a "clothes stick" and rinsed. Ruth was thrilled when the family bought a washing machine that had to be turned by hand. Ironing was just as cumbersome, with most clothes needing to be starched and ironed.

Fortunately, all work and no play was not the philosophy of Ruth's parents. The Kiesels were a musical family. Both George and Christine Kiesel played the harmonica and loved to sing. Ruth's mother would often dance around the house, though her father never cared much for dancing. Ruth sang "The Yellow Rose of Texas" with her father and listened to her grandmother sing Danish songs.

When Ruth was old enough to work in town, she got a job in a grocery store. At night, she did what work was left for her at home, mostly washing and ironing. After two years in high school, she had to quit to help her mother, who was expecting twins. The school principal tried to persuade Ruth to return to school the next fall, promising her a teaching job when she graduated, but she declined the offer, a choice she always regretted.

Ruth moved to Salt Lake when she was nineteen, working in the bakery at Lipman's Grocery Store. She soon became manager of the department, working there until her marriage to Wilford Jensen of Ephraim, Utah, on February 4, 1918. When Wilford was drafted in World War I, shortly after their marriage, Ruth returned to her job at Lipman's. In September she gave birth prematurely to a daughter who lived only twelve hours. Wilford returned from the war, and they settled in Ephraim.

Ruth lost two more children in the next three years. On August 31, 1925, which Ruth described as "the happiest day of my life," she gave birth to her daughter Dorothy, the current owner of so many of her mother's quilts. Two more daughters were born to Ruth, one of them dying at the age of five.

Ruth was a widow for the last thirty-four years of her life. She quilted, played with her grandchildren, quilted, crocheted a bedspread, quilted, worked in the Manti L.D.S. Temple, quilted, worked as a housekeeper in the L.D.S. mission home in Minneapolis, and quilted. The embroidered "Pansy Quilt" with its graceful basket medallion and wide contrasting border, quilted all over with clamshells, was made as a wedding gift for her daughter.

1946

Basket of Flowers

75" x 86"

Cotton

Made by Ruth Delila Kiesel Jensen

(1897–1986)

Made in Ephraim, Sanpete County, Utah

Owned by Dorothy Stoddard

Inez
Oman
Critchlow

Price, Utah, was originally settled in 1879 by Caleb Rhoades and brothers Frederick and Charles Grames. Those early settlers and their families suffered food and water shortages that made the first pioneering attempt especially difficult. In 1883, with the coming of the railroad to the Castle Valley town and the opening of nearby coal mines, Price became a center for education, business, and politics and the uniquely diverse community it is today.

Twenty-two-year-old Judson Dorse Critchlow came from Pennsylvania to Price in October 1904 to run the farm his father had bought from a Mormon missionary in need of funds. The growing town of Price at that time had a post office, a small store, and a doctor's office. Dorse became a respected and successful farmer and cattleman on his father's land.

In 1910, Dorse fell in love with eighteen-year-old Inez Oman, whose family had recently settled on a farm next to the Critchlow place. She was the second of twelve children born to Andrew and Celestia Draper Oman. Inez and Dorse were married in Price in 1912 and became the parents of eight children. One son and a pair of twins died before reaching adulthood.

Inez and Dorse settled on the Critchlow farm, where Dorse had not yet added electricity or running water, but Inez was used to hard work. As a child, she had cooked in a sheep camp for hungry shearers. She quickly mastered all the chores necessary to run a self-sufficient home and farm, from making butter and raising chickens and turkeys to butchering hogs and rendering lard for cooking purposes.

Quilting and embroidery were Inez's hobbies. She made more than fifty quilts in her lifetime, giving them to her children and grandchildren. The Iris Applique quilt she gave to her son John and his wife, Sophia, in 1947 is an exquisite example of her superior quilting talent. The quilt was made from a kit purchased in Salt Lake City at ZCMI, often called "America's first department store." Inez appliqued by hand the pink, violet, peach, and gold irises and their green stems and leaves, using her tiny trademark stitches that made the sewing virtually invisible. She did not do the actual quilting, but directed the progress of the L.D.S. Relief Society quilters like a general commanding his troops. She had always done the same thing whenever she quilted with Sophia, watching over and commenting on her daughter-in-law's every stitch.

Twelve irises float in the center of this ethereal quilt and a dozen single buds dance around them. In each corner seven flowers burst through the white background in shades of purple, pink, peach, and yellow. A curling, waterlike design quilted onto the top evokes the fluid, tranquil feeling of flowers floating on a surface of shining water. A green binding finishes the scalloped edges of the gift Sophia has treasured for nearly fifty years.

1947

Iris Applique

72″ x 83″

Cotton

Made by Inez Oman Critchlow

(1892–1981)

Made in Price, Carbon County, Utah

Owned by Sophia Critchlow

Alice
Elizabeth
Mellor
Lloyd

Twenty hoop-skirted, parasol-twirling colonial ladies stroll through the gardens of this captivating scrapbag quilt made in 1947 by Alice Lloyd. The ladies were a favorite pattern of Grandma Lloyd, according to her granddaughter Jean Olsen; she also embroidered and appliqued them on dresser scarves and pillowcases. She even danced the faceless ladies across the top edge of a sheet by embroidering them from the waist up, then adding a full crocheted skirt to each one.

The Colonial Ladies pattern is only one example of the pictorial quilts that caught the fancy of so many quilters in the mid- to late 1920s. Pictorial quilts were essentially appliqued pictures, repeated across the surface of the quilt and set together with fabric sashing. Traditionally, the shapes were outlined with an embroidered buttonhole stitch. Alice Lloyd's Colonial Ladies is a unique representation of this particular quilt type because she used an outline stitch to attach the appliqued pieces. Other pictorial patterns such as Sunbonnet Sue, Scotty Dogs, Coverall Bill, and Butterflies were immensely popular when this quilt genre reached its pinnacle in the 1930s.

Alice Lloyd was sixty-seven when she made this wedding quilt for her oldest grandchild, Jean. She had spent a lifetime honing her sewing skills. Alice also made a Dresden Plate quilt, many Sunbonnet Sues, an Irish Chain, and several Nine-patches, as well as numerous "canyon quilts" to be used for camping and picnics. Jean still keeps a pile of old Nine-patch squares in the sewing basket that once belonged to her grandmother, squares pieced on a treadle sewing machine but not yet stitched together.

The fabrics for the Colonial Ladies and Alice's other quilts came from scraps, usually left from the aprons she made for her daughters, nieces, and granddaughters on their birthdays and at Christmas. Alice was of the old school of thought and believed that quilts came from scraps, not from the store. Her husband was a miner and a miner's wife with six children never wasted what could be used elsewhere.

Alice was a fun-loving and cheerful woman, despite her prim appearance. She always wore a long-sleeved, high-collared dress and black boots that laced halfway up her calves—"nine-inch boots," she called them. Her braided hair was long enough to sit on before she wound it around her head into a tidy bun each morning. She wore a corset until the day she died at age eighty-nine.

Alice's granddaughter Jean began quilting some twenty years ago with a group of like-minded friends who had tried every other imaginable craft. The quilting struck an inner chord with Jean, perhaps reminding her of the many evenings she spent as a child watching her Grandma Lloyd embroider, crochet, and piece. Jean specializes in hand-pieced quilts, but has never attempted to make the pictorial quilts her grandmother enjoyed so much.

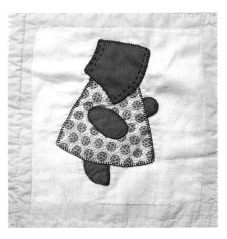

Detail
Sunbonnet Sue
Made by Phoebe Boman Pitcher
Owned by Mildred Olmstead

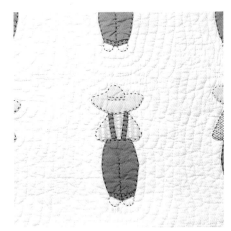

Detail
Sunbonnet Sam
Made by Jessie Franklin Loofbrow Ross
Owned by Marilyn Kirkpatrik

Detail
Sunbonnet Sue
Quiltmaker unknown
Owned by Fay Nilsson

1947

Colonial Ladies

58″ x 72½″

Cotton

Made by Alice Elizabeth Mellor Lloyd

(1880–1969)

Made in Spanish Fork, Utah County, Utah

Owned by Jean Olsen

Detail
Scotty Dogs
Made by Evelyn Nebeker
Owned by Louise Gordon

Pauline
Waddoups
Jensen
Luckey

Pauline Luckey began her quilting career when she was twelve years old, and has pieced more than fifty quilts in her lifetime. The first was a Sunbonnet Sue baby quilt with blanket stitching around blocks her mother had sewn onto bleached flour sacks. One of her most recent creations is a Double Wedding Ring completed in January 1995. Pauline remembers playing beneath quilts-in-process when she was small, while her mother and friends quilted overhead.

Pauline was born in Dayton, Idaho, to F. W. and Annie Jane Page Waddoups. She had four older sisters and two younger brothers. In 1942 the family moved to Utah where she met and eventually married Roy Jensen in Ogden, Utah. Roy and Pauline settled in the little farming community of Corinne.

Corinne, Utah, is a town with a past steeped in folklore so flamboyant and questionable that the truth may never be sorted out. Known variously as "The Burgh on the Bear," "The City of the Ungodly," "The Chicago of the West," and even "Sodom," the city was a product of the railroad boom of 1869. As the Union Pacific and the Central Pacific railroads raced to their historic meeting at Promontory Point in early 1869, a group of non-Mormon army officers and merchants were building their "Gentile city" six miles west of Brigham City, certain that it could compete financially and politically with established Mormons in Utah. Corinne was the last town built along the Union Pacific right-of-way, bringing with it an interesting assortment of pickpockets, entrepreneurs, criminals, miners, and ladies of the night. After one year, Corinne boasted 1,500 citizens, 500 buildings, and town lots selling for a thousand dollars. Plans for the city were detailed and ambitious, including land set aside for a University of Corinne. When the railroad center was moved from Corinne to Ogden in the late 1870s, the city changed into the quiet farm town it is today.

From 1946 until 1950, Pauline cut, pieced, and stitched fabric scraps for her beautiful Dresden Plate Flower motif. She gave each plate a yellow center and at least one pink and one blue piece. She had seen the pattern on other quilts, but wanted hers to be different, so she added solid green stems and green print leaves to make the plates look like flowers. She learned to use her new Belaire Zigzag sewing machine by stitching around the pieces in black. When she started joining the finished blocks together, she decided to turn them different directions, creating a very distinctive design. The quilting was done by a Mrs. Biggs of Franklin, Idaho, a neighbor of Pauline's sister. She quilted the outlines of the pieced shapes and stitched flowers and circles where the squares meet. The pale yellow border is quilted in a beautiful feather design.

In 1959, at the age of thirty-three, Roy died of colon cancer, leaving Pauline and their four children. Two months after his death, their fifth child, a son, was born. Pauline says of this time, "I thought it was the end of the world." But life went on and so did the quilting. Five years later, Pauline married Alvin Luckey of Corinne.

Cataract surgery on both eyes has not kept Pauline from her quilting. She is thrilled to be recognized for the handiwork she has created.

1946–1950

Dresden Plate Flower

77½″ x 89½″

Cotton

Made and owned by Pauline Waddoups
Jensen Luckey (1927–)

Made in Corinne, Box Elder County, Utah

QUILTS—VOICES OF WOMEN PAST

The Quilt without a Story

Jeana Kimball

Throughout this book you will find well-documented accounts of quilt-makers and their quilts. Unfortunately, few quilts have survived for several generations with this information. Quilt making was such an ordinary and common practice in earlier generations that not many people thought it was important to record who made these everyday bedcovers. After all, quilts were made strictly for warmth. Or were they?

Quilts were often made from leftover bits of fabric from homemade clothing construction and parts of worn clothing that had some wear left in them, such as the top of a gathered skirt.

It was a virtue to waste nothing. The old saying, "Use it up, make it do, or do without" was practiced daily in frugal Utah households. As a fifth-generation Utahn, I remember well the recycling of worn clothing into quilts by both my mother and her mother. One of my last memories of my Grandmother Hoyt was visiting her while she sat on the edge of her bed cutting out squares for a quilt top. That day she said to me, "I don't know who will use this, or when it will be finished, but it seems such a waste to do nothing." She died two months later. To the very end she was concerned with not wasting time or fabric. That quilt was finished by my mother, and it now belongs to my daughter. In spite of its humble appearance, to Emily it is a treasure created by her grandmother and great-grandmother.

Most would consider something made from recycled and leftover fabric as having little or no value. What we forget is that the woman who stitched those scraps together left behind a record of herself: her choice of pattern and color preferences, as well as her needle skills. A woman in previous generations had little opportunity to create great works of art. Her role was that of wife, mother, housekeeper, and seamstress. Usually, her only avenue for artistic expression was through her home and the things used in it. She was further limited by a lack of abundant resources to work with.

When beginning to make a quilt, a quiltmaker had a series of choices to make. She could choose from a variety of patterns. By choosing a particular pattern she revealed something about herself. If her quilt blocks were made from simple square shapes, she may have been showing her efficiency in completing the piece in the shortest time, or perhaps she liked the tidy shape of the square pieces. Were her favorite patterns made primarily of half-square triangles (a square cut in half diagonally)? Maybe she liked the twinkle of somewhat irregular shapes. Whatever she chose, she was making a statement about what was visually pleasing to her.

A quiltmaker usually had a scrapbag containing a variety of fabric. She often increased her fabric choices by trading similarly sized pieces of fabric with her friends and neighbors. She may not have had numerous color choices, but while using what she had, she chose how it would best blend with the others. As she chose which fabric to place in each position on a pattern, she was making color decisions. Once again, when she laid out the blocks for joining them into a quilt top she was making decisions about color and balance. Often a quiltmaker would add bright or contrasting fabric in strategic places to create visual rhythm or to sparkle across the quilt's surface.

Her choices of batting and backing were also important decisions. What was available for the inner filler? Store-bought cotton batting, or wool, carded from last spring's shearing, or another well-worn quilt to be recycled as batting? For the quilt's backing fabric she may have had to buy new fabric to get pieces large enough. If so, did she choose on the basis of cost, visual appeal, or both? Or, did she carefully take apart empty sugar, flour, and feed sacks and then stitch them together as a whole to create a piece large enough for the quilt's backing?

As the quilting pattern was chosen, she was again making decisions. Did she have time to lavish tiny, even stitches in an intricate pattern? Or was the quilt needed soon? If so, stitches were less fine and the individual quilting lines were spaced further apart.

Even though little factual information is known about the woman who made the very worn quilt pictured here, there is much to be learned about her by examining the quilt closely.

I believe it was made as a special occasion quilt, perhaps as the maker's wedding quilt. The crowning touch to a woman's trousseau was the completion of her bridal quilt. She would buy all new fabric, the best that she could afford, to make this special quilt. Her bridal quilt, whether pieced, appliqued, or a quilted counterpane, was intended to display the maker's "coming of age" and to demonstrate her skill with a needle. The completion of her wedding quilt indicated a young woman's readiness for marriage and mature responsibility. Appliqued quilts, such as this one, were rarely, if ever, made for everyday use. The time involved in hand stitching the top alone would have been several hundred hours. That investment of valuable time was not meant to be used up in a few short years.

This unique applique design was no doubt created by its maker as a statement of visual beauty. In the course of research I have done, I have found that no two applique quilts are exactly alike. Each quiltmaker created her own version, sometimes following a typical format or layout of the pieces, but always with something unique to make it her own. "Foundation Flower" is the format of this block layout. Traditional names for elements used in this quilt are "poinsettia" or "sunflower" for the big red and orange flower in the center of each block and "tulips," both large and small, on the stem ends. I have not seen another quilt with this unique combination of components.

Notice the fine green line that separates each block from the others and how it is also used to separate the body of the quilt from its border. That green line is tiny piping, carefully created and painstakingly placed for visual effect. It was a task far above the ability of an average or impatient needleworker.

Hundreds of hours were invested in the quilting. Tiny, fine quilting stitches (ten to twelve stitches per inch) were skillfully used to create unique and varied quilting patterns on both the top of the appliqued shapes and to closely cover all the background areas between the applique motifs. Its preservation is due to the fact that heavily quilted quilts wear much more slowly than ones with minimal quilting.

Martha reveals much information about herself in this 85¼" x 87" bed-covering: she was infinitely patient, a highly skilled needlewoman, and detail oriented. Martha's quilt was meant to display her best side, the one that she wanted others to see. Is her worn quilt worth preserving? Emphatically, yes. It represents so much of who Martha was.

Go back to the beginning, and as you look at the quilts in this book, read and think about the women who made them. Each quilt, in its step-by-step creation, speaks for its maker—her voice is clearly there, between the fabric and lines of stitches.

1878

Tulip with Vine Borders

85¼" x 87"

Cotton

Made by Martha Steel

No information has been found about her,

who she was, where she lived

Owned by the Uintah County DUP

Museum, Vernal, Utah

AUTHOR'S NOTES ON THE WRITING OF *GATHERED IN TIME*

In a very real sense, the stories for this book were harvested like ripe fruits from an opulent garden. The hopeful "gardeners" of the Utah Quilt Heritage Group had tilled and sowed, watered and weeded the fertile soil of that garden since 1988, hoping for a bumper crop that would reflect the state's rich quilting history. For six years, dedicated volunteers worked to document more than 2,200 Utah quilts. They measured lengths and widths, counted the number of quilting stitches per inch, determined whether quilt batts were cotton or wool, identified fabric content, labeled embroidery stitches, and cross-referenced quilt patterns. Most important, from my point of view, they asked the quilt owners to write a brief history about the maker of their quilt, supplying information about birth, marriage, death, family life, education, ancestry, employment, places of residence, anecdotes, and anything else the owner thought pertinent about the maker. When the documentation was completed, a number of quilts were chosen for inclusion here using specific criteria. The quilt must have been made in Utah prior to 1950 or must have come to Utah with the early pioneers. Most of the counties in the state should be represented, and there should be a wide variety of quilt types and patterns. And finally, the quilt must have a story to tell.

Most of the quiltmakers in this book passed from this earth long ago, with no one left to remember the small details of their lives. Consequently, the majority of these stories were pieced together from family histories and genealogy. Some families provided volumes of information about their predecessors, information which required careful pruning and cutting to uncover the important and relevant parts of the story. Other families knew only names and dates, but like a seed buried deep in the ground, even those stories began to emerge. For those quiltmakers still living, the process was somewhat easier, but not always; they were often most reluctant to talk about themselves. Those busy women would rather have been talking about the last quilt they made or the one they would soon begin.

Interviews with the quilt owners were held face to face in their homes, with the exception of a few that were conducted over the telephone. My method of questioning was simply to try to fill in the holes that occurred in the brief histories I had been given. Those short biographies became the path I followed as I walked through the garden. If not enough was known about the quiltmaker, I looked to local or state history or the story of the quilt pattern itself to provide some insight into her life and times. I traveled from Smithfield in northern Utah to St. George in the south and most counties in between to see and touch each quilt and look into the eyes of the owner as she—or he, for many of the quilts are owned by sons and grandsons—talked about the ancestor who had sewn the heirloom quilt. Many times the interview became an emotional, tearful tribute to the woman who had devoted so many hours making a quilt the family now cherished. I often marveled that an old and worn bedcover could be so valued, but it seemed to be a physical connection with the past, a bond of love beyond time and across the generations.

My overwhelming impression of these past eighteen months with the Utah Quilt Heritage Group is one of generosity—the generosity of the members in inviting me into the garden and giving me the tools I needed to complete the harvest and, as well, the generosity of the quiltmakers and quilt owners who opened their homes and hearts to me so that I could tell the stories of these wonderful Utah women and their quilts. The seeds were planted, the harvest is in, all is gathered in time.

Acknowledgments

The Utah Quilt Heritage Board is grateful for the help of so many wonderful people, most of all to the many volunteers at Documentation Days. Board members helped arrange facilities, publicity, sometimes meals and housing, and then furnished the energy and enthusiasm to work through the Days. Volunteers provided the fabric and helped plan, piece, and quilt the five quilts that were raffled to extend our meager funds. Seven thousand volunteer hours were recorded, and there must have been at least that many more.

The National Quilting Association provided a small grant as the work began. Many interested persons and organizations graciously donated money: Jean Christensen, Paul and Jeanne Huber, Keith Tripp, the Deseret Foundation, the L.D.S. Hospital, the Allstate Foundation, the Utah Pioneer Sesquicentennial Celebration Coordinating Council, the Utah Quilt Guild, the Great Salt Lake Area Quilt Group, and various other Quilt Guild chapters throughout the state. The George S. and Dolores Doré Eccles Foundation gave its support with two substantial grants to the Utah Quilt Heritage Corporation. Without its generosity, the publication of this book would not have been possible.

A sizable portion of the cost of publication was defrayed for us by Interwest Graphics, Inc., who made the color separations without charging for labor, for which we are very grateful.

Without the donated services of Christian P. Anderson and of Holme, Roberts and Owen, it would have been impossible to overcome the snarls of red tape along the path.

In 1988, the original Utah Quilt Heritage Board included Marguerite Allen, Dick and Gayle Frandsen, Betty Roberts, Eugene and Margaret Talbot, and Eunice Young. This is the group that began the labor of documenting many, many quilts. As the years passed, some members left the board and others took their place: Carol Bunyard, Pat Hansen, Jeanne Huber, Ruth Moon, Bill Ormond, Joyce Robison, and Saundra Tripp.

Kae Covington, author of this book, had no particular knowledge of quilts when she began to gather the stories of the quiltmakers. She has come to love quilts and has developed an appreciation of them through research and personal interviews with the families of the quiltmakers. Kae has a way of talking to people that often awakens a memory which adds life to a story. We appreciate her hard work and thank her family for the loan of Kae for more than a year.

Laurel Dokos, the photographer, brought out the best in all the quilts. Some of the much-loved, much-used, and tragically faded ones were a challenge, but they all look their best due to her expertise. Thanks to Vicki Johnson-Mischler, Laurel's assistant, for keeping track of the pictures of the quiltmakers.

Dr. Dean L. May, Utah historian, author, professor of history at the University of Utah, was kind enough to write the Introduction, which we hope will foster among people outside of Utah some understanding of the "peculiar people" who founded this state.

We owe a debt of thanks to Eunice Young for writing the Preface. She was present at the beginning and it seems fitting to have her words as the project ends.

We appreciate Jeana Kimball's writing about the need for documentation. It is indeed a tragedy when the story behind an old quilt is lost. Jeana is internationally known as a teacher, designer, and writer, and we feel fortunate to have her share her knowledge with us.

The map in the front of the book is the work of Raef Porter. As the list of place-names grew, we realized a reference map was needed, and he drafted one for us that includes some modern towns along with some very old ones that were not easy to place.

Members of the Utah Quilt Heritage Board who are currently tying the last knots and clipping the final threads are not the same group who began, so please forgive us if we have not mentioned your assistance. This project has been lengthy—growing, shrinking, and changing as it moved along—but every person and every hour donated is deeply appreciated, even if not mentioned individually.